THE GOD-KINGS
OF OUTREMER

by

Hugh Montgomery

The Book Tree
San Diego, California

© 2008
Hugh Montgomery

ISBN 978-1-58509-119-5

Interior layout: Atulya Berube
Cover layout and design: Daniel Flood
Map, chart & original document enhancement: Daniel Flood

Cover Illustrations, from top, clockwise:
Mary with Jesus as King; Mary, Joseph and the twins;
the seal of the Knights Templar—two knights on horseback which supposedly
indicated poverty but may, in fact, have indicated a knowledge that Jesus was one
of twins.

Published by
The Book Tree
P O Box 16476
San Diego, CA 92176
www.thebooktree.com
We provide fascinating and educational products to help awaken the public to new ideas and
information that would not be available otherwise.
Call 1 (800) 700-8733 for our *FREE BOOK TREE CATALOG*.

To Hermione, my wife, who cast her spell over me

Also by Hugh Montgomery

The God-Kings of Europe: The Descendents of Jesus Traced Through the Odonic and Davidic Dynasties

The God-Kings of England: The Viking and Norman Dynasties and Their Conquest of England (983-1066)

Table of Contents

Acknowledgments 6

1   The Beginnings of the Jigsaw 7

2   The Abdias Manuscript and the Petra Dynasty 15

3   The Dynasty of the Black Madonna, The Herodians and Saul 33

4   The Descendants of Jesus' Brothers and Sisters 41

5   The Zadokites, The Zealots and the Sicarii 45

6   The Benjamites, an Elite Fighting Force and the Joms-Vikings 51

7   The Varangian Guard 57

8   The Normans and the Kingdom of Sicily 61

9   The First Crusade and the Establishment of Outremer 69

10 Kingdom of Jerusalem & Formation of the Knights Templar . . .89

11 The Angevins 101

12 The Odonic Line Again 105

13 The End of the Kingdom of Jerusalem & the Knights Templar .117

14 Appendices A-U 123

15 References, Sources and Further Reading 179

14 Index 187

Acknowledgements

I must once again acknowledge a debt of gratitude to my cousin Sophie Montgomery in Sweden, who provided me with copies of the Arundel and Belvoir documents and cartulary of Rouen from the collection of her late father, Count Bo-Gabriel de Montgomery, and for checking and answering many questions from the wonderful documents and books in her father's collection. Also to members of the Sinclair Open Forum, who have sent me nuggets of information and to Shawn Sinclair, who is running the Ulvungar DNA project. To those academics from all over the world, who have patiently answered my questions and where necessary have translated ancient manuscripts for me. To the curators of the Norris and Fordham University collections in the United States, who have allowed me access to their collections of ancient manuscripts, as well as curators of the Hamsfort, Regis Danorum, Tischendorf and Liber Burgundorum collections in Europe. If I have inadvertently forgotten a name please excuse my error of omission.

Chapter 1

The Beginnings of the Jigsaw

In my books *The God-Kings of Europe* and *The God-Kings of England* I charted the origins of the great Ulvungar Dynasty. I showed how they originated with the marriage of Ataulf of the Visigoths with Maria of the Elchasaites. How they became the rulers of Scandinavia, then Normandy and eventually Kings of England. This book will continue their saga, but first we need to go back in time to the fourth century whence the dynasty arose.

In AD 318 a group of eight men arrived to see Sylvester, Bishop of Rome, now designated "Pontifax Maximus" or Pope by the Emperor Constantine. They were the heads of the eight families descended from Jesus and his relatives. They are known to history as the "Desposyni." With them they brought copies of their most precious documents, their families' genealogies and their versions of the Gospels. They demanded of Sylvester that their hereditary Bishoprics of Jerusalem, Antioch, Alexandria and Ephesus be kept strictly within the family and that any Bishops to these ancient Sees appointed by Rome, should be withdrawn. They also reminded Sylvester that unless a Bishop had received the "laying on of hands" from James, the brother of Jesus or one consecrated by him then they were not a true Bishop. They also demanded that the tithes that had traditionally been sent to Jerusalem for the upkeep of the Hebrew or Judaic-Christian Church be resumed.

Sylvester informed them that they and their relatives were to be written out of the history of the Church. In future the Church would be the One and Only Church of the Roman Empire, with its spiritual head to be the Pope based in Rome and its secular head to be the Emperor based in his new Capital of Constantinople (then still called Byzantium). The tithes in future would be paid to Rome. Their Genealogies and Gospels were declared non-canonical and only Bishops consecrated by Rome were to be considered legitimate. They were dismissed back to their native lands. Where you may ask does

7

this information come from? From no less a person than the Jesuit Professor, Malachi Martin.(1) Malachi Martin was Jesuit professor at Rome's Pontifical Biblical Institute and helped translate the Dead Sea Scrolls. He was a personal friend of many Popes and had access to all the Vatican's Secret Library documents.

In AD 325 the Emperor called a Council of the Church in Nicaea to decide definitely on the Canon or Dogma of the Church. Athanasius argued for Jesus to be declared equal to God. The Ante-Nicene Fathers produced the genealogies and a copy of St. Mathew's Gospel in Hebrew, which clearly showed that Jesus had married and had children. They posed the question, "If Jesus is Divine are his Children?" There was of course no possible answer! A Bishop called Arius suggested a compromise whereby Jesus was to be declared similar to God but not identical. Eventually the anti-Nicaeans (to distinguish them from the Ante-Nicaean fathers) fell in behind this compromise by Arius, but Athanasius would have none of it. The Emperor, fed up with the protracted discussions, came down on the side of Athanasius and had a document drawn up, which became known in due course as "The Nicene Creed." He then sent it to each Bishop to sign under penalty of death. Most signed but some escaped and refused to sign. Later Eusebius, who wrote *The History of the Church*, and was, it appears, on good terms with the Emperor, persuaded the Emperor to recall Arius and when Athanasius refused Arius communion, the Emperor exiled Athanasius.(2)

But the damage had been done. Jesus' real genealogy was written out of the Canon of the Church and a rather clumsy compromise of a trinity of Father, Son and Holy Ghost imposed instead, with a virgin birth straight out of Roman and Greek religious mythology and a resurrection from the same source. Compare Zeus impregnating Europa in the form of a Bull, Jupiter impregnating Leda in the form of a Swan and God impregnating Mary in the form of the Holy Spirit. Compare also the Roman Emperors being declared Gods and ascending into heaven and you get the picture.

But how did this come about? Constantine I had become Emperor in 308 AD. It is doubtful that he himself was ever a believing Christian, but he had a mother called Helen or Helena. She had been born a slave in Bithynia and at some time had converted to

Christianity, at that time very much a religion of slaves and servants, who even if their life on earth was hell, could aspire to a life of heavenly pleasures after death. She saw the chance with her son becoming Emperor, not just to stop the persecutions of the Christians, but the chance to make Christianity *The Religion* of the Roman Empire and I expect nagged poor Constantine until he agreed to talk seriously first to Sylvester's predecessor, Miltiades, and when that was rejected, to Sylvester, when he in turn, became Bishop of Rome. In return for Sylvester making some changes to the Christian theology, Constantine would make him Pontifax Maximus and give him the Lateran Palace to live in and a large stipend from the state. In fact it was Constantine, who called a meeting of Church leaders and informed them that he, Constantine, accepted and accredited Sylvester as Miltiades successor. The alternative for Sylvester would have been what had happened to many of his predecessors – He could be sent to the lead mines where they would put out one eye and fill it with lead, castrate him and hamstring him. Life expectancy was six months. It is hardly surprising that Sylvester chose the former.

But Constantine also saw this as a way of controlling the people's religious life as well as their physical life. This would give the State control over every aspect of a citizen from birth to death and beyond. Sylvester in turn saw this as a way of expanding the Christian message to the whole then known world.

In my book *The God-Kings of Europe* I showed that there existed documentary evidence for Jesus being married and having descendants and that these descendants had married into the Visigothic Line of Kings, who claimed descent from Odin, the God of Norse Mythology, but who in fact had been a real person. From this line there sprang a dynasty called the Ulvungars who had ruled much of northern Europe for centuries.

I had traced, at that point, only one line from Jesus, but was there more? In 318 AD there had been at least eight lines from either Jesus or his brothers and sisters. Was it, I wondered, possible to trace some or all of the rest? This book is about the quest to try to put the bits of the genealogical jigsaw puzzle together and to see what happened to the main line.

Since I published *The God-Kings of Europe* I have received copies or photographs of a number of documents that I mentioned in *The God-Kings* and we shall be examining some of these further in this book. Furthermore I have been contacted by a number of people taking part in a vast DNA project, which appears to prove the documentary evidence.

This is what one of the leaders of this study wrote:

"You're bang on! In essence, in accordance with the central theme and evidence that you put forward in your book, it has become quite evident that there was a deliberate effort over the past 2000 years to control/facilitate the strategic intermarriage of those descendents of the Odonic and Davidic dynasties. All of which culminated around 1000 AD in the various French Royal/Ducal Houses including Normandy." (3)

It would appear that a large number of the Sinclair Clan members (whom I have shown were one of the main Ulvungar families) show not only Nordic lines of descent but also the Jewish Cohen/Levite Modal Haplotype including, in some cases, up to twelve separate markers. Now I confess I do not understand the science of DNA and have to therefore accept what others, who do, tell me (see Appendix A). It seems likely however that the DNA studies confirm the documentary evidence I produced in *The God-Kings of Europe*. What was interesting was that there appeared to be more than one line. It was going to be difficult to investigate all of them so I had to start with what documentary evidence there was.

There are four documents that show that Jesus was either married and or had children. The first is *The Gospel of Philip* – part of the Nag Hammadi documents written in Sahedic Coptic around 150 AD. However there is a Greek fragment of these same documents, which has been dated to between 50-75 AD, making this as old as or older than any of the Canonical Gospels. On the next page I give a photograph of the relevant page from *The Gospel of Philip*. As can immediately be seen it states quite clearly that Jesus had both a special "Companion" (Koinonos) and "Wife" (Koinonos). Koinonos is used in the Sahedic Coptic, via Greek and the verb Koinonum, meaning to copulate with or to mate with, and Koinonos means "sexual partner."

There is absolutely no possibility that it means some form of platonic friendship.

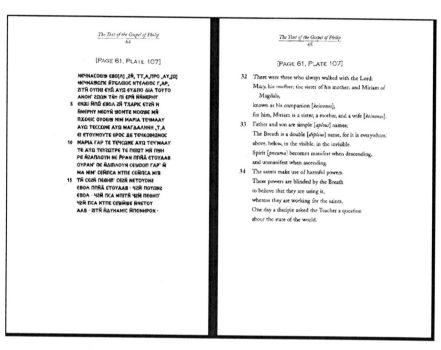

Ref: 4

The second document is known as "The House of Bethany" and is a Latin document from the early fifth century. In fact, it can be dated to between 412-430 AD. (For full explanation of the dating see Appendix B.)

Maria et Jesu Maria genuit. Maria et Sigismundus Ruth et ejus frater genuit. Ruth et Osmeus Elchasius genuit. Elchasius Marthana et Martha genuit. Maria ex semene sancto Elchasius biro Ata nubit. Maria et Ata Clodomirus genuit. Clodomirus Merobus genuit.

Ref. 5

Translation: "Mary and Jesus produced Mary. Mary and Sigismundus produced Ruth and brother. Ruth and Osmeus produced Elchasius. Elchasius produced Marthana and Martha. Maria of the seed of the blessed Elchasius married the man Ata. Maria and Ata produced Clodomirus who produced Merovus."

There are a number of interesting things to notice about this document. First and foremost the woman's name comes first, not the man's. This would be almost unthinkable in medieval society and yet this is emphasised by making the verb third person singular. In other words *she* rather than *they* produced. The only people to whom descent from the mother is paramount are the Jews. If your mother is Jewish and your father isn't, you are Jewish, but if your father is Jewish and your mother is not, you are not Jewish. Clearly this is a Jewish Genealogy at least in origin, though the second part from Clodomirus may well have been added at a later date.

In *The God-Kings of Europe* on page 41 I produced a genealogy based upon this document.

There are two further documents – *The Legend of Mary Magdalene* (Appendix C), which is in fact about Mary of Bethany, and a fragment of a document that may be the Latin translation of a Hebrew or Syriac original. These documents are given in English in *The God-Kings of Europe*.(6)

References
Chapter 1

1. Martin, M. (1981), *The Decline & Fall of the Roman Church*, pp. 41-44, G. P. Putnam's Sons, New York. Also Eusebius, trans. Cruse (1998) *Ecclesiastical History*, p. 21 Hendrickson Publishers, Inc., MA.

2. http://www.bible.ca/history/fathers/ANF-08/anf08-66.htm 17/05/2006 *Ante-Nicene Fathers* Vol. VIII. See also Montgomery, H. (2006) – *The God Kings of Europe*, p. 9 & App. II, The Book Tree, San Diego, CA.

3. E-mail from William Mann, USA, dated 20th November 2006. See also Appendix A – Cohen Haplotype.

4. LeLoup, Jean-Yves, *The Gospel of Philip*, p. 65, Inner Traditions, Rochester, Vermont.

5. House of Bethany – Burgundian Documents (Liber Burgundiorum), private collection. A copy came into the possession of William Montgomery sometime in the 17th Century and it now turns out that a further copy was in the possession of Dr. Hugh Sinclair (See Chapter 2).

6. Montgomery, H., op. cit., pp. 124 & 162.

Chapter 2

The Abdias Manuscript and the Petra Dynasty

Just after publication of *The God-Kings of Europe*, I reached an agreement with the curator of the Norris Collection to receive a photocopy of the entire Abdias manuscript. So far as I am aware the Norris collection has the only complete copy of this manuscript anywhere in the world, so I feel very privileged to now have a copy myself.

Who was Abdias? If you go to the Catholic Encyclopaedia on-line it will tell you that he was a semi-mythical figure whose real name was Obadiah. Well true, but not the whole truth! His name was more correctly Obadas and he was a member of the Royal House of Petra. He was consecrated as the first Bishop of Babylon, though based initially in Edessa, by the Judaic-Christian Church of Jerusalem and was probably installed either by Thaddeus or Judas. Julius Africanus says "he was related to the Lord." (1) On page 8, I have shown the probable genealogy of the Petran Royal House. However for those who have not read *The God-Kings of Europe*, the fact that John the Baptist is shown as marrying into this house and becoming effectively its Crown Prince by way of his wife may come as a surprise. In my book *The God-Kings of Europe* I postulated that John the Baptist had been a member of the Petran Royal House or at least related to them, and that Mary Magdalene had been his daughter.

It is now worthwhile looking at this in more detail to see what real evidence there is. The House of Petra was more usually called the Royal House of Nabatea and the Nabateans were part of the great Semitic-Arabic population of the Arabian Peninsula. There were two groups to this population, the Sabeans or Southern group based at Saba (possibly the Biblical Sheba) and the Nabateans or Northern group based at Petra. Both were great trading nations – the Nabateans controlling most of Palestine, Syria and Lebanon prior to their annexation by the Romans, and the Sabeans in the first century AD controlled not just the Southern Routes but their Empire extended well into what is now Ethiopia and included the hill fortress of Magdala.(2) It is probable that the Falashas of Ethiopia were converted to Judaism at the same time as the Petrans or Nabateans, rather than being descended from the Queen of Sheba, as they claim, but it is easy to see how they would have this legend. After all, Saba is simply another name for Sheba. Indeed if you look at the Falashas' beliefs, they mirror very closely the ideas of the Petran Zadoks, which are mentioned hereafter. They did not celebrate Hanukkah, which celebrates the rededication of the Temple in Jerusalem by the Maccabees, and neither did the Petran Zadoks. They knew nothing of Talmud or Misnah, both of which occurred after the fall of the Jerusalem Temple. They did not speak Hebrew any more than the Nabateans or Sabateans. They did not observe the customs concerning mezuzah or phylacteries, neither did the Petrans. They did however keep the dietary laws very strictly and they celebrated Passover (Pessach) by sacrificing a lamb on 14th Nisan. Interestingly, the Book of Amos says that the Israelites were at one time in Ethiopia or Cush. Amos 9:7 says, *"Are you not as the children of the Ethiopians unto me, O children of Israel? saith the Lord. Have I not brought up Israel out of the land of Egypt?"* There appears therefore to be a long- standing relationship between Israel and Ethiopia, indeed Moses' wife was supposed to be a black Ethiopian (see also Appendix A). Was John the Baptist deliberately likening himself with Moses and was Jesus doing the same? (For full details on the Falashas' beliefs see Encyclopedia Judaism under Falashas.)

John was known to be a member of the Essene community and many scholars regard the title used in the Dead Sea Scrolls, "The Teacher of Righteousness" as referring to John. But there was another group or groups, who were associated with the concept of "Righteousness" and indeed their names may well have been simply another name or names for the Essenes. These were the Zadokites, *zadok* meaning "righteous" in Hebrew, and the Zealots who were "zealous in obedience to the Law." Michael Baigent in his book *The Jesus Papers* suggests that Jesus' family may have been Zadokites.(3)

We know from the work of Strabo, the 1st Century Roman historian, that in Nabatea, with its capital at Petra, there was a colony of Essenes (The Esser sect of the Jews). Petra is in modern Jordan, which takes its name from the River Jordan, where of course, John famously baptised Jesus. It seems likely therefore that John was part of this community. On page 9, I have given the probable genealogy for John, which you will note is a bloodline of Zadok priests, who incidentally did not accept the Temple in Jerusalem as being the authentic Temple, but regarded the Temple in Egypt as being the only true Zadok Temple.(4)

From the Canonical Gospels one is led to believe that John spent time in the deserts in Israel, but did he? As both a Zadok and married to Anya (5) he is more likely to have gone first to Egypt and then on to Ethiopia. Married to the daughter of King Aretas, he may well have gone on what amounts to a Royal Tour to show himself to the people, as heir presumptive, in the name of his wife, of the Sabean/Nabatean Empire. This may well have taken several years, and he would have been accompanied by Anya, because his position was only as a result of his marriage. It is not unlikely therefore that a daughter was born to them in Magdala, who in due course became known as Miriam of Magdala, translated into English as Mary Magdalene. Indeed the name "Miriam" may even be a title. According to Robert Morcot, the priestess daughters of the nobles of Egypt and Ethiopia under the Black Pharaohs, were called Chantresses to the Lord of Miam, or Mi-ri-am.(6) She is also called of the House of Aethiopia in at least one document.(7) Tore Kjeilen suggests that Jesus may well have spent his young childhood in the Nabatean Kingdom and it is therefore not unlikely that he met Mary Magdalene there.(8)

Many people assume that Magdala was the place 120 miles north of Jerusalem on the Sea of Galilee. Its full name was Magdala Taricaea, meaning the Tower of Fish. However, I have a problem with this. This village was destroyed by an earthquake or something similar, attributed to an Act of God because of the people's fornications, according to the Hebrew Text, *Lamentations Raba*. It is probable that Mary's identification with prostitution came from this association. This village was not around in 7 BC to 7 AD and was not rebuilt until very much later; indeed it was only found again in about 1800 AD.

I shall be using the spelling Aethiopia, literally *the land of the burnt face people* in Greek, for the people of North Africa and the Arabian Peninsula, which is how it would have been used in the 1st Century, whilst Ethiopia denotes the geographical area more or less of modern Ethiopia.

The official reason for John's beheading by Herod, that of *Salome and the dance of the veils*, has always seemed to me to be a story concocted to cover up the reality. Let us look at some historical facts. In 31 BC the Nabateans lost a large chunk of their kingdom, carved out by Rome, to Herod the Great. The Nabatean Kings were not happy with this state of affairs and King Aretas married his daughter to Herod Antipas, Herod the Great's son and Tetrach of Galilee, with the understanding that any son of theirs was to become Tetrach after Herod Antipas and thereby bring Galilee back into the Nabatean fold. A Tetrach was the ruler of a fourth of a Roman province. According to Josephus, in his *Antiquities of the Jews,* Herod Antipas was in the process of divorcing his wife, King Aretas's daughter. She got wind of this and fled to her father in Petra. Aretas was furious and mounted a military operation to overthrow Herod Antipas. John was also furious, not so much because of Herod's wishing to marry someone else's previous wife, but because Herod's wife was his sister-in-law. I believe Herod took John as a hostage and when his forces were defeated had John's head cut off in revenge. Indeed, it may well be that John was stirring up the Jewish population to overthrow Herod Antipas and perhaps replace him with John himself. This seems much more likely to me. It is important to realise that John, as I have shown in *The God-Kings of Europe*, was not just a few months older than Jesus, but several years older as the Mandean documents attest. This can also be shown because according to Torah nobody could teach in the Temple unless they were married and nobody could become a priest unless he had produced a child. The Pharisees insisted on a male child. Yet John's father was supposedly already a priest at the time of Mary, Jesus' mother, becoming pregnant and he apparently had been a priest for some time. As all sources agree that John was their only child, it follows that John must have been considerably older than Jesus, probably about 14 years older.(9)

It must be remembered that the Herodians were hated by the Jews. "Herod the Great" was only called that by his cronies, to the Jews he was "The Edomite Slave." He was Idumaen and supposedly converted to Judaism via circumcision, however Herod Antipas was Herod's son by a Samaritan woman and therefore not a Jew.(10) To be a Jew one's mother must be Jewish, as I have stated before.

The point about all of this is that Obadas/Abdias was related to both John the Baptist, perhaps was even his son, and via Mary Magdalene to Jesus by marriage. It is worthwhile pointing out that it was to Petra that James and the Jerusalem Church fled for refuge with their families when the Romans sacked Jerusalem. Whatever therefore Abdias wrote must be taken very seriously indeed. A genealogy of Jesus and his brethren by Abdias is more likely to be accurate than any of the canonical gospels, which were written later and are known to have been rewritten to conform to Church doctrine.(11)

The Petra Dynasty

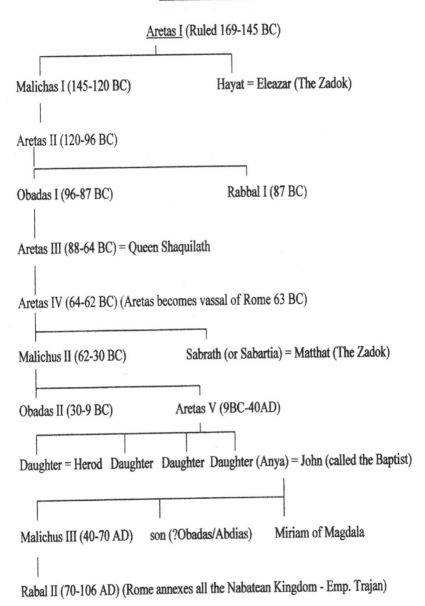

Aretas I (Ruled 169-145 BC)

Malichas I (145-120 BC)   Hayat = Eleazar (The Zadok)

Aretas II (120-96 BC)

Obadas I (96-87 BC)   Rabbal I (87 BC)

Aretas III (88-64 BC) = Queen Shaquilath

Aretas IV (64-62 BC) (Aretas becomes vassal of Rome 63 BC)

Malichus II (62-30 BC)   Sabrath (or Sabartia) = Matthat (The Zadok)

Obadas II (30-9 BC)   Aretas V (9BC-40AD)

Daughter = Herod   Daughter   Daughter   Daughter (Anya) = John (called the Baptist)

Malichus III (40-70 AD)   son (?Obadas/Abdias)   Miriam of Magdala

Rabal II (70-106 AD) (Rome annexes all the Nabatean Kingdom - Emp. Trajan)

Although the above is tentative, it is with my present knowledge, the most likely, though Abdias could be the son or grandson of any of the four daughters except Herod's wife.

Probable Zadok Dynasty

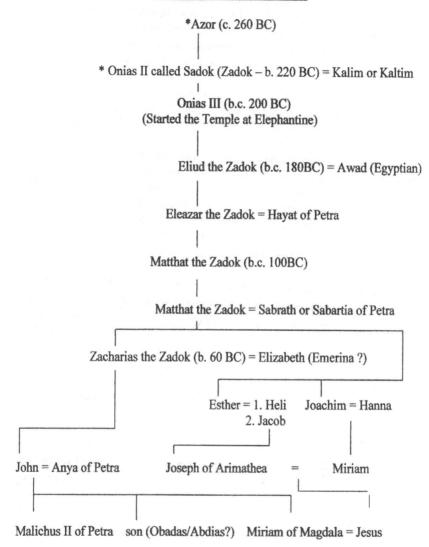

*Azor (c. 260 BC)

* Onias II called Sadok (Zadok – b. 220 BC) = Kalim or Kaltim

Onias III (b.c. 200 BC)
(Started the Temple at Elephantine)

Eliud the Zadok (b.c. 180BC) = Awad (Egyptian)

Eleazar the Zadok = Hayat of Petra

Matthat the Zadok (b.c. 100BC)

Matthat the Zadok = Sabrath or Sabartia of Petra

Zacharias the Zadok (b. 60 BC) = Elizabeth (Emerina ?)

Esther = 1. Heli   Joachim = Hanna
        2. Jacob

John = Anya of Petra   Joseph of Arimathea   =   Miriam

Malichus II of Petra   son (Obadas/Abdias?)   Miriam of Magdala = Jesus

* When was Onias I? Was Azor - Onias I?

Although the Zadoks appear to have been an hereditary priesthood as was normal in Israel, it did not necessarily go from father to son. One should therefore be wary of calling this a genealogy although it is probably a bloodline. It is also likely as a consequence that there are generations missing.

The first marriage between the Zadok Dynasty and the Petra dynasty took place somewhere around 150 BC, after the Petrans had been converted to Judaism. It seems likely that this Zadok dynasty became the High Priests of Petra and may well have opposed the Temple Priesthood in Jerusalem. Recently excavations in the mountains near Petra have uncovered what appears to be an open air temple type structure, which would accord well with the Zadokite ideals.

The Idumeans, Galileans and Nabateans had all been forcibly converted to Judaism by the Hasmonean rulers, though there is some disagreement amongst scholars as to whether only the elite were converted or whether all of the Nabateans were Jews.(12)

Again, for those who have not read my previous book it may come as a surprise that Joseph of Arimathea is shown as being identical with Joseph, the husband of Mary, but there is ample evidence. The Family of Jesus was taxed in Rama (Graeco-Roman Arimathea), James the Just (Jesus' brother) is "ha Rama Theo" and in Mathew 2:18 it says, "In Rama there was a voice heard lamenting," supposedly over the death of the babies on Herod's orders. Why Rama? Because Jesus' family came from there! (13)

So what does Abdias say about Jesus and his brethren? In book six it says:

"Simon Chananaeus cognomine, ac Iudas, qui & Thadaeus, & Iacobus, quem fratrem Domini quidam appellant."

(Simon known as Chananeus, also Judas, who together with Thadeus and Jacob (James), are called the brothers of the Lord). It goes on:

"Fratres germani fuerunt."

(They were real brothers or by blood). It also says that Simon is called Chananaeus because his mother, the second wife of Joseph, was called Chana and was Galilean.

In book nine it says:

"Beatum Thomam ...ipsumque a Domino Didymum, quod interpretatur geminus."

(The Blessed Thomas ... himself Didymus to the Lord, which is to be interpreted as *his twin*). (Didymus is anyway Greek for twin and Thomas comes from the Hebrew/ Aramaic word for twin.)

From Abdias we can therefore start to build up a family for Jesus:

Jesus – Judas/Thomas – Jacob (James) – Simon (Chananaeus) – Judas (Judah) – Thadaeus

Plus we know from other sources that he had two sisters, Joanna and Salome. He also had a full sister, Mary (see the *Gospel of Philip*). I have put after *Thomas* the name Judas in brackets because, according to the *Gospel of Thomas*, he was called Thomas Judas Didymus.(14) Is Abdias referring to the same person in books 6 and 9? The problem is the Latin translation of Jude, Judah and Judas may equally have been translated as "Judas." Generally speaking it is agreed that Jesus had a brother Judah, so for the time being I am going to suppose that there are two brothers, one called Judah and one called Judas (Thomas, his twin). There was also, of course, James the Just (or Jacob), who later took over the Jerusalem Church. Simon is also referred to as "Petreus," as opposed to "Petrus." It is very easy therefore to confuse Simon-Peter (Petrus) with Simon the Petran (Petreus). In fact, in the *English New Testament* I fear that Simon-Peter and Simon the Petran may well have been muddled up on more than one occasion.

We therefore have the following known connections:

A. 1st Century AD (According to Abdias & Others)

Jesus – Judas (Thomas) – Jacob – Simon (Chananaeus -The Petran) – Judas/Judah – Thadaeus – Joanna – Salome

B. 4th Century AD (According to M. Martin -15)

Zacharias – Joseph – John (Jonas or Joachim) – Jacob (James) – Joses – Simeon (Simon) – Matthias – Joshua(?)

Was it possible to work out who descended from whom?

In *The God-Kings of Europe*, one line of descent from Jesus had already been shown, via his daughter Miriam, which had resulted in the Jacob who is mentioned in B, above (16):

<u>**Fig. 1**</u>

<u>**Elchasaic Line from Jesus (God-Kings of Europe p. 154)**</u>

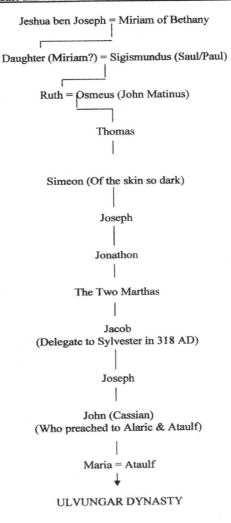

Jeshua ben Joseph = Miriam of Bethany

Daughter (Miriam?) = Sigismundus (Saul/Paul)

Ruth = Osmeus (John Matinus)

Thomas

Simeon (Of the skin so dark)

Joseph

Jonathon

The Two Marthas

Jacob
(Delegate to Sylvester in 318 AD)

Joseph

John (Cassian)
(Who preached to Alaric & Ataulf)

Maria = Ataulf

ULVUNGAR DYNASTY

But there were other lines, according to Malachi Martin. In his book *The Decline and Fall of the Roman Church*, he says on page 42:

"There were at least three well-known and authentic lines of legitimate blood descendants from Jesus' own family. One from Joachim and Anna, Jesus' maternal grandparents. One from Elizabeth, first cousin of Jesus' mother, Mary, and Elizabeth's husband, Zachary (Zacharias). And one from Cleophas and his wife, who also was a first cousin of Mary."

Let us look at this statement a little more carefully and in particular the statement that there was a legitimate line of descent from Zacharias and Elizabeth. Luke Chapter 1 verse 7 states that Zacharias and Elizabeth were childless and stricken in years. They only had the one son – John the Baptist – therefore, any descendants of theirs' must be descended from John and of course the name of one of the people who went to see Sylvester was John, a family name.

We know that there was a Petran dynastic continuation, but was there more? Did Abdias marry, or was there another son? Importantly, if Mary Magdelene was John the Baptist's daughter, and everything points to this, then there exists considerable evidence that she married Jesus or was his concubine, though now I am fairly sure that she was one of his wives – so what of their children?

Is this, then, the well-known and authentic bloodline to which Malachi Martin refers?
Is this the bloodline that, as Martin puts it, "Was never emphasised by the Popes?"
What a wonderful Jesuitical understatement!

In my book, *The God-Kings of Europe*, on page 147 I quote a source for the "Family of Jesus 5." This is comes from the work of Dr. Hugh Sinclair, who died about thirty years ago and who, besides being one of the foremost scientists of his day, was also the Sinclair family genealogist.(17) It is also mentioned in a somewhat obscure Celtic legend that Jesus went to or lived on Iona (18) from where I had taken the information. Let us therefore examine this statement carefully.

What is interesting is that Dr. Sinclair came to the same conclusions that I did, but some forty years earlier – including that John the Baptist was Mary Magdalene's father and that John was a member of the Royal Petran Dynasty, though it is not clear from his scribbling if he thought that John's father was also a member of that dynasty or whether, as I believe, that John became its Crown Prince through marriage. As we shall see later on, this suggests that the Sinclairs are one of the families that hold or held certain ancient documents, which, as we shall see, became a major reason for the Ulvungar dynasty's conquests.

I have been able to find documentary evidence for a John Matinus (cognomen Osmeus) being the son of Jesus and Mary Magdelene and I assume that John Martinus and John Matinus are one and the same.(19) If indeed Mary Magdalene's father was John the Baptist, and he was now dead, it is quite likely that they had a son called John. It is also probable that they had a daughter called Sarah.(20) Sinclair says that John Martinus married twice, first to a woman called Elizabeth, by whom he had a daughter called Sarah, who in turn had a daughter called Sarah Bernice. Secondly, he married a woman called Muriel by whom he had two sons, Thomas and Germane. (21)

Fig 2

John the Baptist's Line (According to Dr. Sinclair)

Black line of Nabatea & Pharoahs

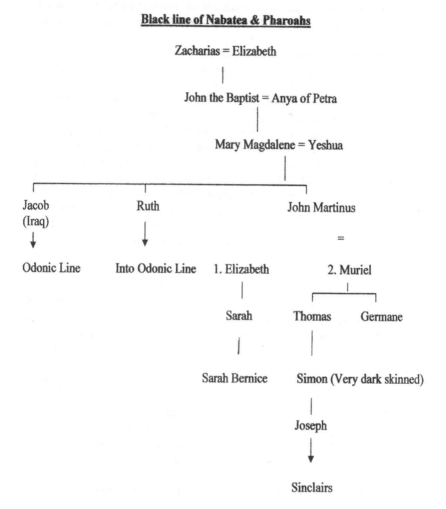

As mentioned, we have evidence that there was a person called John *Matinus*, (cognomen Osmeus), who was the husband of Ruth, the grand-daughter of Jesus and Mary of Bethany, and he appears to have been a descendant of John the Baptist.(22) It seemed likely that John Martinus and John Matinus were one and the same. Matinus seemed to have an association with Matins – the first prayer of the day in monas-

teries or the first order of the new day – and it occurred to me that
Matinus might indicate a new beginning for the line of John the
Baptist's, perhaps the first in line.

However this gives us a problem. According to the *Bethany
Document*, Osmeus married Ruth, but, according to Sinclair, Martinus
married Elizabeth and Muriel. On the other hand, both Dr. Sinclair's
line and the *Bethany Document* show a Thomas, a Simon or Simeon,
who is dark skinned, followed by a Joseph and both lines lead eventually to the Sinclairs. Yet, Sinclair's genealogy had a sister for Martinus
called Ruth, which also went into the Odonic line, whilst my research
showed a sister called Sarah. The name Muriel was originally a code,
whilst the name Ruth came from the *Bethany Document*. What I think
we are seeing is that Dr. Sinclair had scribbled these down but had
needed more time to investigate further. For the time being, therefore,
and until it is proved otherwise, I am going to take the position that
John Martinus, Matinus and Osmeus are one and the same, that his
wives were Ruth and Elizabeth and that he had a sister called Sarah
and a brother called Jacob – all of which fit in my own researches. For
the names Sigismundus, Osmeus and Muriel see in Appendix under
"Codes of Protection."

There are a number of things to note. First, the name Thomas probably only means twin, just as Jesus' twin brother Judas became known
as Thomas, so I would expect that this Thomas's real name was John
and that Germane is simply an anglicised form of Germanus, Latin for
brother, or a miss-spelling of Geminus, the Latin for twin. As twins
tend to run in families, it would not be surprising if Jesus and Mary
Magdalene's daughter-in-law also had twin sons.

Osmeus Martinus, the youngest son of Jesus and Mary Magdalene,
married the grand-daughter of Jesus and Mary of Bethany, his half-
niece. This was not an unusual occurrence. This, then, ties in the two
lines and shows the first interweaving of family bloodlines. As we
shall see, this will be by no means the last time. It also explains where
"Simon, of the skin so dark" comes from – the dark-skinned Madonna,
Mary Magdalene, of the House of Petra and Aethiopia.

The fact of the matter is that there is considerable difference of
opinion between scholars and genealogists. Part of the problem is the

muddle between Mary of Bethany and Mary Magdalene and which completely obscured everything for so long. The other problem is names. Some got changed or errors were made in copying, but sometimes we do not know if a name is a personal name or a title. For example, *The Golden Legend* says of Mary Magdalene that she owned the Castle of Magdalo and was descended from a line of kings. Unfortunately, it then goes on to muddle her up with Mary of Bethany. Nonetheless, there are sufficient clues in this work to show that it and the so-called *Legend of Mary Magdalene*, quoted in my book *The God-Kings of Europe*, are based upon the same source.(23)

In fact, I suspect that the good bishop, Jacobus, wrote *The Golden Legend of Mary Magdelene* to counter the original one, which was certainly circulating in the south of France and possibly Italy. The two are given in full in Appendices C & D, so that the readers can see for themselves how one derives from the other.

1. In Appendix C: "A priestess of the Goddess from the village of Bethany."
In Appendix D: "Martha had her part Bethany."
2. In Appendix D: "And this is she, that same Mary to whom our Lord… showed so great signs of love. He embraced her all in his love, and made her right familiar with him. He would that she be his hostess."
In Appendix C: She "…was affianced to a man called Jeshua… Now Jeshua was of the house of David and they were married."
3. In Appendix D: "They came to Marseilles."
In Appendix C: "So Miriam took ship and was secretly smuggled into Gaul."
4. In the story of *The Golden Legend* it is the king and his wife who want a child, sacrifice to the Goddess, and are cursed by Mary Magdelene. In the second version of this tale it is the king who takes Miriam's daughter against her mother's wishes and it is he who is cursed by the goddess.
5. In both cases, Mary protects and brings up a "little child."

However, whilst Appendix D is full of ridiculous miracles, typical of the Church's belief in magic, the second is rather more restrained, though it, too, has its curse whose conditions must be fulfilled.

There is also quite clearly a relationship between the House of Burgundy and Mary of Bethany or Magdalene in *The Golden Legend*. If you look at the Genealogy of the ancient Gothic kings, as found on page 20 in *The God-Kings of Europe*, the relationship is clearly shown. In the first, the Duke is called Gerard of Burgundy, in the second it is Gundahar of Burgundy, whose daughter marries into the line of Bethany. Once again, events have become telescoped, as frequently happens with legends.(24)

References
Chapter 2

1. Eusebius, trans. G. A. Williamson, Harmondsworth 1981. Eusebius states that Thaddaeus was Bishop of Edessa c. 90 AD, so he probably invested Abdias.

2. http://9.1911encyclopedia.org/S/SA/SABEANS.htm 27/12/2005. See also LexicOrient (8) below.

3. Baigent, M. (2006), *The Jesus Papers*, pp. 144-150, Harper-Element.

4. Ibid. also Taylor, J. *A Second Temple in Egypt*, Waikato University.

5. Drower, Lady E.S. (1937), *The Mandeans of Iraq and Iran*, Oxford University Press. In one of his love poems to Anya, John refers to her as "The Pearl of Petra." One is forced to rely almost entirely on the work of Lady Drower as successive Islamic governments and finally Saddam Hussein destroyed this unique culture and their books. See also Montgomery, H. (2006), *The God-Kings of Europe*, p. 37, The Book Tree, San Diego, CA.

6. Morkot, R.G. (2000), *The Black Pharaohs*, p. 81, Rubicon Press. Dr. Hugh Sinclair's researches suggest that the Petran Royal Family may be related to the Black Pharaonic dynasty of Egypt, see fig. 2.

7. Montgomery, H. *op. cit.* p. 32.

8. Kjeilen, T. (2006, *LexicOrient*. Also published on http://i-cias.com/e.o/nabateans.htm.

9. Drower, *op. cit.* Also Montgomery, H., op. cit. Deuteronomy Chapter 23 verse 1, which more or less mirrors Torah, states that nobody who is incapable of producing a child may be counted within the people of Israel. The only way this could be proved in the time of Jesus, was by marrying and fathering a child. Another good reason why Jesus must have fathered a child, as otherwise he would not have been allowed, as an adult, to take part in Jewish worship.

10. McFarlan, D.M. (2005), *The Dictionary of the Bible*, Geddes & Grosset.

11. Montgomery, H. *op. cit.* p. 27. For the flight to Petra see Martin, M., note 14, below.

12. Dimont, M.I. (1962), *Jews, God & History*, pp. 88-90, Signet Books; Josephus, *The Jewish War*, 1:87, trans. G. A. Williamson (1981), p. 40, Josephus 1:61 (p. 48), 1:363-377 & 377-391. See also Wikipedia under Nabateans. See also Kjeilen, T. (2006), *LexicOrient*.

13. Ibid. See also Document 1 in Montgomery, H., *op.cit.* p. 32.

14. *Gospel of Thomas* (2005), trans. Leloup, J-Y. p. 9, Inner Traditions, Rochester, Vermont. This is also confirmed by the *Acts of Thomas* in the

New Testament Apocrypha in which Jesus himself says, "I am not Judas called Thomas, I am his Brother." – *Acts of Thomas*, 8:11.

15. Martin, M. (1981) – *The Decline & Fall of the Roman Church*, p. 42 –43, Putnum's Sons, New York. Refers to those who visited Sylvester in 318 AD.

16. Montgomery, H., *op. cit.* p. 154.

17. After the publication of *The God-Kings of Europe* I received a copy of this scribbled genealogy from Maj. Niven Sinclair, who had found this amongst the genealogies and papers of the late Dr. Hugh Sinclair and which he had given to Maj. Sinclair. Dr. Hugh Sinclair had been Churchill's nutrition expert during WWII and had founded the International Nutrition Foundation to whom he left his entire estate upon his death. His extensive library and genealogical collection was subsequently sold to the State of British Columbia. Woodrow Wyatt called him "The greatest living scientist."

18. Ford, D. N., (2006), *Early British Kingdoms*. http://www.earlybritishkingdoms.com/articles/josanc.html 15/12/2006.

19. Montgomery, H., *op. cit.* p. 32.

20. Ibid.

21. Genealogy by Dr. Hugh Sinclair, also Montgomery, H., *op. cit.* p.147.

22. Montgomery, H., *op. cit.* p. 154.

23. de Voraign, Jacobus (1275), *Aurea Legenda,* Edited Ellis, F. S. (1900), Temple Classics. Montgomery, H., *The God-Kings of Europe, op. cit.* p. 124.

24. Montgomery, H., *op. cit.* p. 20.

Chapter 3

The Dynasty of the Black Madonna, The Herodians and Saul

As we have seen from the previous chapter, Mary Magdalene was almost certainly black and it would not be surprising if she and Jesus had a black child or children.

In the church of St. Maries de la Mer there is a statue of two women in a boat – The Two Marys. The one on the left is dressed in blue with a gold cloak and has dark hair, the one on the right in red or pink with a blue and red cloak with gold embroidery and has gingery-coloured hair. The one on the left holds a jar and there is another jar beside the one on the right. In the crypt there is a Black Madonna statue that is worshipped by the Gypsies and is called Sarah. Sarah is supposed to have arrived with the two Marys in the boat and is called by the Church – a servant.

Let us look at the likely reality! In Church iconography Mary Magdalene is always shown wearing red – either a red dress or a red cloak and is shown with red or gingery hair. We can therefore make the reasonable assumption that the one on the right is Mary Magdalene. So who is the one on the left? I suggest Mary of Bethany, Jesus' other wife. Both wear the girdle of a married woman. The one on the left holds a type of enclosed chalice and there is another enclosed chalice at the side of the one on the right. What could these chalices signify? Perhaps they are indications of the presents given to Jesus at his birth, perhaps they also indicate a chalice, a bit like the one in which the 'Host' is kept. As the "Host" is supposed to be the "Body" of Christ, is this a coded way of telling us that they are carrying the "Body" (e.g. child) of Jesus? If so, then the one on the left would be indicating that she is pregnant with that child, as she is holding the chalice in her hand, in front of her body. The second one, with the chalice beside her, is indicating that she has already given birth to that child and that the child is accompanying her.

If so, then Sarah is not a servant but is the one on the right's child, the black daughter of Mary Magdalene. If the other is indeed Mary of Bethany then she is pregnant and would have to give birth in southern France, just as Document 4 in *The God-Kings of Europe* indicates.(1) Once again the Church has tried to hide a legend that is fact, but unfortunately does not conform to Church doctrine.

33

There is a whole literature on the Black Madonnas of which the best are by Euan Begg and Avis & Robert Mander.(2) The most famous are at Montserrat in northern Spain, the black Madonna of Candelaria in Tenerife (Patroness of the Canary Islands), Clermont, Aurillac, Meymac, and Chartres, but there are others in Czestochova in Poland and Belgrade, Serbia, where there is also an icon of a black John the Baptist.

All these statues show a mother and male child, supposedly Mary (the Virgin) and Jesus, but more likely Mary Magdalene and her son John. But as I have shown above, her daughter Sarah also had children. The problem I found, as I started to research further, is that there are any number of so-called lines of descent from Mary Magdalene, most of which do not agree with each other. There is work by Roderick Stuart (*Royalty for Commoners*), and work by Dr. Michael Poynder. There are letters written by Eleutherius to King Lucius, circa 184 AD, and then there is the *Aurea Legenda*, all of which make claims about Mary Magdalene.(3) However, I believe that Fig. 3 is the most likely at the moment. In particular, I believe that the two lines of Jesus and Mary of Bethany, and Jesus and Mary Magdalene intermarried and that it is that mixed line that survived.

There is some evidence for this proposition. The first of these is the names of the Herodian Dynasty and, in particular, the name Bernice. As can be seen from the Herodian Dynasty genealogy, Aristobulous marries a Princess (Sarah) Bernice, the niece of Herod the Great, and their granddaughter is called Bernice. If we then look at the Genealogy of Saul/Paul and see that he is related to the Herodians, we can start to see a picture of from where the names came.

The Black Madonna Dynasty Fig. 3

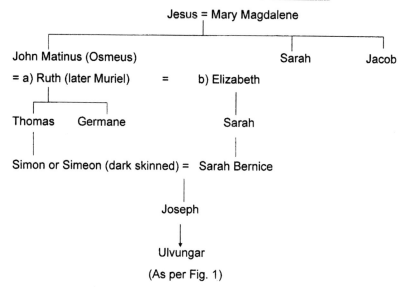

Jesus = Mary Magdalene

John Matinus (Osmeus)   Sarah   Jacob
= a) Ruth (later Muriel)   =   b) Elizabeth

Thomas   Germane   Sarah

Simon or Simeon (dark skinned) =   Sarah Bernice

Joseph

Ulvungar

(As per Fig. 1)

Herodian Dynasty (4)

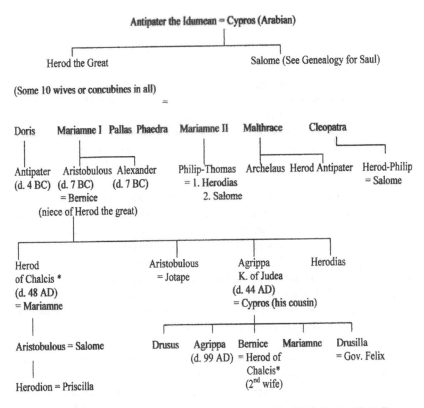

According to one source Antipater (d. 4 BC) had a child by his father's wife Pallas (5).

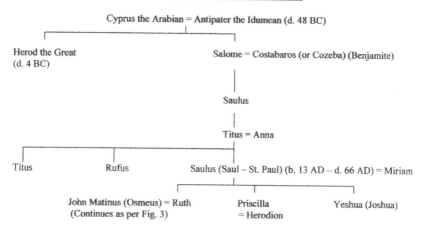

Genealogy for Saul (later St. Paul)

It is possible that more than one line from Mary Magdalene survived and had descendants but I have so far been unable to find any reputable research that shows it. Lawrence Gardner in his book *The Bloodline of the Holy Grail* makes various claims of descent. The problem is that he has Mary of Bethany and Mary Magdalene as one and the same person, and some of his genealogies that I have checked, such as that of the Franks, do not agree even with the sources that he himself quotes.

However, there are some interesting snippets of history that may bear out this line of descent. The Valois have always claimed descent from Mary Magdalene and at least one Queen of the Valois dynasty had a black child. Now everyone assumed that it had been fathered by a black dwarf that the Queen kept as a servant and of whom she was very fond. The story goes that the attending doctor or midwife said that the black birth had been caused by the dwarf's stare, to which the king is supposed to have replied, "It must have been a very penetrating stare." There is a painting by Velasquez showing the Queen and her black dwarf. The Queen however always protested her innocence. Was she perhaps innocent after all? Did the black Magdalene gene surface again?

Then there is the question of the son of King Edward III called "The Black Prince." This was supposedly because of his "Black Armour." However, there exist detailed records in the Public Records Office of all of the Prince's armour and not once does the record mention "Black Armour." For example, for 1338 the record shows: 1 Harness; 2 Bascinets; 2 Pieces of Plate Armour; Poleyns; a pair of Plate Gauntlets; a pair of Armpieces; 1 Pisane; 1 Ventail; Vambraces & Rerebraces. In other words, this list entails a complete suit of armour and a spare helmet, yet none are shown as "Black."(6) However, both Froissart and the French call him "Dark Visaged." Was he in fact very dark-skinned?

It is also obvious that at least some of the Royal Families of Europe were and still are very well aware of their own descent, why otherwise would the Orléans branch of the Spanish Royal Family call a prince, *Ataulfo*. (Prince Ataulfo de Orléans, cousin of King Alfonso XIII).

But what of the descendants of Jesus' brothers and sisters?

References:
Chapter 3

1. Montgomery, H. *op. cit.* p. 124.
2. Begg, E., (2000), *The Cult of the Black Madonna.* Mander, A & R, *The Black Madonna* (2002), published privately.
3. Eleutherius was Bishop of Rome 175-189 AD; he was born in Nicopolis, Greece.
Lopes A., (1997), *The Popes*, p. 5, Futura Edizoni, Roma.
Taylor, J., (1969), *Letters of Eleutherius to King Lucius.*
Aurea Legenda: The Golden Legend or Lives of the Saints, by Jacobus de Voraigne, Archbishop of Genoa 1275, First Edition 1470, English Version by William Caxton, First Edition 1483, Edited by F. S. Ellis, Temple Classics, (1900).
Internet: *Medieval Source Book*, Fordham University Center for Medieval Studies.
Gardiner, L., *The Bloodline of The Holy Grail.* Poynder, M., *Mary Magdelene*, as yet unpublished. Begg, *op. cit.*
4. McFarlan, D. M. *op. cit.* p. 101-103.
5. Pope, C. N., (2005), *Herodian Identities of New Testament Characters*, see http://www.domainofman.com/book/sup5.html 23/05/2007.
6. Barber, R., (1978), *Edward Prince of Wales and Aquitaine*, p. 21, The Boydell Press. See also Public Record Office 101/387/25 m. 27.

Chapter 4

The Descendants of Jesus' Brothers and Sisters

In Chapter 2, the list of Jesus' brothers and sisters is given as follows:

Jesus (Yeshua) – Judas-Thomas (his twin) and Jacob, both full brothers and Simon, a second Judas (or Judah or Jude) and Thaddeus as half-brothers, and Salome and Joanna as sisters, though it is not clear whether they are full or half-sisters. It is probable that Judas-Thomas became known as Thomas to distinguish him from the half-brother Judas. There may have been other brothers and sisters as outlined in Chapter 11 of *The God-Kings of Europe,* but for the purposes of this chapter, I am going to use only those documented by Abdias and supported by other sources as well.

Let us deal, first of all, with Jesus' twin brother, Judas-Thomas, because we know a surprising amount about him. We know he was born on the same day as Jesus, probably in the year 7 BC. And that he died after 80 AD in India and was buried there, but later his bones were dug up and returned to Edessa. Why Edessa? Because he had been based in Edessa at the beginning of his "ministry" and had married a daughter of King Abgar of Edessa (probably Abgar IX), one of whose daughters was called, in Greek, Melusine.(1) They had two known children, Evodeus (born 25 AD – died 68 AD) and Theophilus (born 30 AD – died 107 AD). From Evodeus descends Theoderet (b.c. 57 AD) and then Bardaisan (b. 154 AD in Edessa), though there may be a generation missing. Bardaisan died in 222 AD in Armenia and there is possibly a direct descent to the king of Ani, the principal Armenian Ruler of the early 11th century. Theophilus also had a son born about 60 AD, but we do not have a name for him, nor do we know much about his descendants.

It seems likely that Judas-Thomas had to move out of Edessa when the Romans took over and take refuge in India, almost certainly with his twin brother, Jesus. They could not possibly have stayed on in territory controlled by Rome. In fact, according to the *Acts of Thomas,* Jesus himself went to Edessa and then on to India with Judas-Thomas. But there was also Jesus' half-brother, Thaddeus, who appears to have gone with Judas-Thomas to Edessa, possibly to install Abdias as

Bishop of Babylonia, and to have stayed there. We do not know who he married, but if his brother married a daughter of King Abgar, it is possible that he did, too.(2)

James or Jacob the Just, Jesus' other full but younger brother, also married. He married his half-aunt, Mary-Cleopas, and they had a daughter, Anna, who in turn married Bron-Baruch. Bron was one of the Essene fathers and the word baruch is Hebrew for *blessing* or *blessed*. This has been translated into English as *Bran the Blessed*. How he became an Irish legend as a champion of Ireland, had his head cut off and placed to protect England, etc. is worthy of a book in its own right, but cannot form part of this one. However, from Bron Baruch descends Beli and Penardun. Beli is a Benjamite name, so Bron clearly descends from the Benjamite line.(3)

From Beli descends Ewgen, who married back into the line by marrying Aminadab.(4)

There was also another half-brother called Judas (Judah or Jude). We do not have a name for his wife or wives but we do have names for their children, Zokar and Jacob, by one wife and Anna by a second. From the line of Jacob, it is believed descended Joses, one of the people who went to visit Sylvester in 318 AD. We do not have a complete genealogy for this line, but this is the most likely. Zokar also had offspring, namely James and Jude.

I cannot find any documented evidence for Salome having children but this does not mean that she did not. Joanna certainly married John-Mark, according to Thiering, and had a boy, Jeshua (Joshua, who drowned at age 14) and a girl, Esther. Esther in turn married Jacob, her half-uncle and one of the sons of Jesus by Mary of Bethany and which after four generations married back into that same line, when their great-grand-daughter married Joseph, the four-times great-grandfather of Maria, who married Ataulf (See page 154 in *God-Kings of Europe*).

The other half-brother, Simon (Chananeus or the Petran), was born in about 22 AD and also is supposed to have survived a crucifixion in 54 AD. He had a son, Joses, and a grand-daughter, Miriam, who married Mudar ibn Nizor.(5)

As can be seen, most of Jesus' brothers and sisters married and had offspring.

References:
Chapter 4

1. *Acts of Thomas – New Testament Apocrypha.*

2.Muhammed, Abu J., (1972), *Tafsir-Ibn-i-Jarir at Tabri,* Vol. 3 p.197 Kubr-ul-Mar Press, Cairo.

3. Montgomery, *op. cit.* p. 146; also Eisenman and Wise, *The Dead Sea Scrolls*, p. 47.

4. Ibid.

5. Muhammed, *op. cit.* Vol. 3, pp. 190-200.

Chapter 5

The Zadokites, The Zealots and the Sicarii

In Chapter 2 I have shown that it was likely that Jesus' family were Zadokites or Zealots, but is there any more proof? Well, yes there is! Simon Chananaeus is, according to several authorities, also known as "Zelotes" or Zealot.(1) We know from Abdias that Simon was Jesus' half-brother, the son of his father Joseph by Joseph's second wife, Chana. We know also that his half-brother, Judas, was also called "Zelotes."(2) It has also been suggested that Iscariot may mean *Sicarii*, a group of elite fighters or possibly assassins who were trained to oppose the Romans by force of arms.

It is even possible that Judas Iscariot may have been Jesus' own half-brother. At the very least, the family of Jesus is shown not to be "meek and mild," but on the contrary, a family "Zealous for the Law," some of whose members were prepared to take up the sword against Rome. Indeed, Jesus himself urged his followers to "buy a sword." John the Baptist's family, too, were Zadokites. It seems likely that Petra may well have been the centre of the Zadokite movement, opposing both the Pharisaic and Sadduceen factions at the Temple in Jerusalem and believing that only Onias III's Temple on the Island of Elephantine in Egypt was the True Temple.(3)

This group believed in the concept of a Priest-King, Melchizedek, literally, *The King is Righteous*, combining the lines of Abraham, David and Zadok, and we know that Jesus himself was specifically linked to Melchizedek.(4) They also believed in an apocalyptic vision that was about to happen, when the Angels of the Lord would descend and help the Righteous expel the Romans from Israel.

If we now look at what happened in Gethsemane from this perspective, a very different picture emerges. What was actually to happen? We know that there were armed men there. One cut off the ear of a servant of the High Priest. Why did the Romans send a Cohort and a half (900 men) to capture Jesus? (5) Did Jesus actually go there, just outside Jerusalem, with all of the Zealots believing that the Angels would descend to help them overthrow the Romans? I think he did. But he also knew that if it did not happen then his life would be forfeit, or at the very least, he would have to undergo crucifixion. I believe that he had prepared for that eventuality and because of it, that he survived the Crucifixion.

This is what I think may have happened:
The dates and the stars, according to the Essenes, showed a conjunction that portended the time of the Messiah – but a warrior Messiah – who would unleash the "Dogs of War" and with the help of the Heavenly Host, overthrow the Romans. Everybody would convert to Judaism and God's heavenly reign would begin. This was to happen just after Pessach (Passover).

Barbara Thiering in Chapter 19 of her book *Jesus the Man*, makes clear that Jesus had taken up the position of both king and high priest in preparation for what was to come. He would have celebrated Pessach with his family, because Pessach is very much a family affair. So he would have arranged to celebrate Passover and sent someone to arrange the table and foods beforehand, and would have used a form of service not dissimilar to the present day Haggadah.(6) He would have blessed the wine using the traditional blessings or baruchs. "Blessed be Thou, O Lord our God, King of the Universe, Creator of the fruit of the vine." He would have done the same for the unleavened bread (Matzah) and would have divided it amongst them to eat with bitter herbs. He would have spilt the drops of wine indicating blood, fire and pillars of smoke. The family would have drunk the wine leaning on their left sides.

Who was The Family and who was there? Evidently his father, Joseph, was not, as otherwise he would have headed the table and all authorities seem to agree that Jesus headed the table. His brothers – Judas/Thomas (his twin), Jacob, Thadaeus, Judas (Judah), Simon the Petran and Zealot and five other men – Judas Iscariot (unless he is already family), John, Andrew, Peter and Philip. We don't actually know, because they are not all mentioned in the Gospels. We can assume there would have been ten men to form the "Minyan" (the minimum number of Jewish males present to perform certain ceremonies). Would wives have been present? Almost certainly, but they may not have eaten with the men of the household. Jesus, according to Abdias and the *Gospel of Mary*, is also pretty scathing as to Peter's character. Rather than a rock, he seems to think Peter is a "blockhead" without much moral fibre. *Petrus* is usually translated as *Rock*, but Thickhead or Blockhead would be a perfectly good translation.

At the end of the meal, Jesus asks if they had to pay for anything for the Passover and they say, "No." He then instructs those who do not have swords to go and buy one because the time has now come when the transgressors shall be punished. In other words, they are going to overthrow the Romans. It is obvious that most present already have their swords with them, as shortly afterwards those who did not have swords come back and say they have bought a couple of swords. He had instructed those who did not have swords to go and buy one, and as they only bought two swords, which he says are enough, it logically follows that all the rest already had swords, because when he receives their reply, they leave the room and go to Gethsemane. Why would they do that? The logical answer is that they went to meet others and that these others were also armed. There they wait for what they believe to be the coming of the Lord, but they wait in vain. Eventually, Jesus goes off to pray alone, hoping against hope for the expected arrival of God. Instead, it is the Romans who arrive. Jesus is probably further up the hill when they arrive and initially his followers resist, but when he hears the clash of arms he comes quickly and, knowing resistance is futile, orders his men to put down their arms. The Romans ask, "Who is the leader?" and Judas Iscariot, tears streaming down his face, goes over to Jesus and kisses him, not to point him out to the Romans, but to bid him farewell, believing that this is the last time he will see Jesus alive. We can dismiss the business of Satan entering Judas, etc., as a much later Roman-Christianised version of what happened just as we know from other records that it was the Romans who turned up, not the high priest's soldiers, though there may have been members of the high priest's entourage amongst them. The above has always seemed to be much more likely than the story told by a Romanised Church, which was desperate to hide it's part in Jesus' crucifixion.

Where do I get all this from? My imagination? NO – It comes straight from St. Luke's Gospel, Chapter 22. Read it without the Christian bias taught by the Church and you will see what I mean. However, I believe that through careful planning, Jesus actually survived the crucifixion and that his father, Joseph of Arimathea, played a vital part in helping him. That is why he was not at "The Last

Supper." Plans had to be put in place in case things went wrong. How did they manage it? We don't know, but Barbara Thiering has made some suggestions, as have other authors, but I believe that he was revived from near death and lived to father other children, such as John Matinus.

But the plan of an elite fighting force to oppose the Romans did not end with Jesus, or the concept of a Messiah. We know of the rebellion under Bar Kochba (Simon ben Cozeba (7)) in 132 AD and their eventual defeat, but I do not think that such a strong will to overthrow the Roman Empire, and later its Roman Church, ended even with Bar Kochba. Interestingly enough, Bar Kochba was also proclaimed Messiah by no less a person than Rabbi Akiba, one of the most revered sages of his day. Indeed, Bar Kochba's rebellion united more people that Jesus' ever did and whilst Jesus' relied upon divine intervention, Bar Kochba's was a well-planned soldierly campaign. Bar Kochba himself is supposed to have said to God, "Don't help us too much and whatever you do don't ruin the victory." In truth, Bar Kochba's rebellion very nearly succeeded and Rome had to throw everything into this third Jewish War in order to gain back control of their unruly province. In the process, many Roman Legions were decimated and Rome itself nearly fell.(8)

References
Chapter 5

1. Luke 6:15 & Acts 1:13. See also Martin, M. (2007), *Duodecim Apostoli* http://www.preces-latinae.org/thesaurus/Numeri/Apostoli.html.

2. Ms. 481.51-100, Yale University Collection of Rare Books & Manuscripts, *"Simon itaque Chananaeus et Iudas Zelotes Apostoli."*

3. The Temple to Bubastis on the Island of Elephantine was rebuilt as a Jewish temple in 170 -169 BC by the High Priest Onias III, who had fled to Egypt after his defeat by the Seleucid ruler of Syria. This was, for a time, the only legitimate temple and was always served by an hereditary Zadokite priesthood. They did not accept the rededication of the Jerusalem Temple by the Maccabeans and their continuators, the Pharisees.

4. McFarlan, D. M. *Op.Cit.* p. 177. In Hebrews 6:20 – 7:17 Jesus is specifically linked to Melchizedek. Melche = King, Zadok = Righteous.

5. A Cohort was one-tenth of a Legion, which in turn was 6,000 men in the Roman Army.

6. The Haggadah is the form of service used by Jews when celebrating the Passover meal.

7. A member of the Benjamite/Saulic dynasty, see Genealogy of Saul.

8. Dimont, M. I., (1962), *Jews, God & History*, p. 108-109, Signet Books.

Chapter 6

The Benjamites, an Elite Fighting Force and the Joms-Vikings

In Chapter 4 we looked at the formation of an elite fighting force to overthrow the Romans. In this chapter we shall continue the theme.

In Chapter 4 of *The God-Kings of Europe* I told the story of the Benjamites and their betrayal by the other tribes of Israel, because their form of worship included the feminine Godhead as well as the male. I also pointed out that the Benjamites were probably a separate city-state but that nonetheless, the legend of their betrayal had become a defining part of the Benjamite psyche. They had left Israel and gone to Egypt and had become the famous Elephantine Guard of the Pharaohs, based upon the very island where the High Priest, Onias III, was to set up his Zadokite temple so many years later. Was that the reason for him choosing Elephantine and that temple? Had it once been a Benjamite temple? At the moment we don't know, but it is an intriguing thought. Certainly if you are going to set up your own elite fighters then you need at the very least a tradition upon which to build, and the Zadokite Temple at Elephantine certainly provided that.

So first we have the Benjamite mercenaries at about the time of David, then the Zadokite fighters in around 30 AD, then the Bar Kochba fighters in about 132 AD. Bar Kochba meant *Son of the Star*. Jesus' birth was supposed to be heralded by a star. The significance was not lost on his followers. But now you have a new militant group being formed – Pauline Christianity. Saul or Paul was both a Benjamite and had married the daughter of Jesus and Mary of Bethany and, just like Ali, Mohammed's son-in-law, thought that he and not James, Jesus' brother, should be head of the Cult of Christ. Hence the name changed from Saul to Paul – P from the Greek letters ☧ = Chr(ist). It may well be that Jesus himself supported this. Perhaps there was a sort of conversion from strict Judaism to a reformed type of Judaism, which I think Jesus himself preached. Maybe Paul was, subconsciously, taking revenge for the Benjamite betrayal by changing Judaism into something else.

From this line of Miriam and Paul, you get the line of Ruth, which intermarries into the line from Mary Magdalene. Of course they would

51

regard themselves as being the rightful heirs! But Paul himself was also Roman born and bred and had, at one time, been a Roman Soldier.(1) He and his descendants wanted to convert the Roman and Greek inhabitants of the Empire and were not too worried about them becoming circumcised or keeping strictly kosher. James, on the other hand, wanted to keep to the strict Jewish way of life, so Paul started to be banned from preaching in the synagogues. From this line emerged the line of the Elchasaites.

One might reasonably ask, why then did the Elchasaites go along with all the ablutions and the vegetarianism? But here I see the hand of Mary Magdalene. Jesus would have been old when John Matinus was born and I do not think he had much say in his upbringing. Mary Magdalene, as the daughter of John the Baptist, would have been very much aufait with John's way of thinking and I believe that her son, on marrying Ruth, the daughter of Paul and Miriam, would have influenced the way in which Paul's message was portrayed. However, it must not be forgotten that Paul was himself born into a Pharisaic family, who were the inheritors of the tradition of being apart from the Gentile world and strict keepers of the Law and performance of rituals, including ablutions (indeed, Pharisee means *apart*). One gets the impression sometimes that Paul does not know which way to jump.(2)

It is also worthwhile looking at the name *Elchasai* and how it is made up. It is a lot more obvious in Hebrew.
(M)elche – zai(dok)
In other words, Elchasai is hidden within Melchezaidok and it means *hidden power*. The hidden power of the priest-king! And Jesus himself is linked to Melchezaidok.

Clearly, however, there was disagreement in the Elchasaite fold, one of whose members left to set up his own form of Judaic-Christianity, which became known as Manichaeism. This tried to combine Judaism, Christianity and Zoroastrianism.(3)

I think that their descendants might even have gone along with Constantine and Sylvester had it not been for one thing, the writing out of the Family all together and in particular the obliteration of the direct line of descent from Jesus in Church dogma. This would have been more than Jacob (Paul and Miriam's descendant) could bear. From this point on, it was necessary to form a new elite to fight Roman Catholicism, one being religious and which eventually became the Cathars, and one military. We shall be looking at both of these in the course of this book.

Do not get the impression that Jacob and the leaders of the Desposyni sat down to plot a long term strategy. I do not think they did that. Their first task was to protect themselves and their families because, as Malachi Martin points out, the Roman State deliberately tried to destroy their livelihoods and indeed to kill or otherwise dispose of them. According to this same source many fled, changed their names (see Appendix B) and one or two were reconciled with Rome, or at least pretended to be.(4)

According to Martin, by the end of the 5th Century they ceased to exist as Jewish Christians, but this did not mean that the individual members of those families had all died out, nor that they did not keep their precious genealogies. I think it likely, however, that the Elchasaic line was the only line to survive in Europe, which was one of the reasons it became so vital to protect.

What we see, is them taking whatever steps were necessary for the survival of The Family. The Elchasaites were already a powerful sect with centres in Rome, Palestine, Syria and Babylon and undoubtedly, this sect, with its male/female and good/evil dualistic ideas, became a major tool against Roman Catholicism.(5) However, within a couple of generations another force came into play – The Visigoths.

I have already gone into considerable detail about the Visigoths in *The God-Kings of Europe* and *The God-Kings of England* and do not intend to repeat it here. But with the marriage of Maria of the Elchasaites to Ataulf of the Visigoths, a new chapter in the military opposition to Rome opened up with Alaric and Ataulf sacking Rome itself and carrying away the very treasure which the Romans had taken from the Temple in Jerusalem. Eventually, the Visigoths were themselves forced out of their kingdom in the south of Europe and had to regroup in Scandinavia, where another elite fighting force was formed, that of the Joms-Vikings.

This fighting force was dedicated to the cult of Odin. Its members lived apart from women, in Spartan conditions in barracks where they practiced their fighting skills. Their aim was to die in battle so that they could be reunited with Odin in Valhalla. This was not too different from the Zealots, the later sect of the Assassins and the modern suicide bombers. I have already pointed out the similarities, so far as the followers of Odin were concerned, between Odin and Jesus. Both hung on a tree or cross, both had their sides pierced with a spear, both survived and obtained wisdom and it is easy to see how, with the marriage of Maria and Ataulf, this new fighting force would help protect *The Family*. In *The God-Kings of England* I have shown that Sweyn Forkbeard, leader of the Joms-Vikings, made himself King of England with their help, where they became the Royal Housecarls. Their Norman cousins eventually conquered the whole of England and gave *The Family* and their Jewish members special protection and privileges (6) and, as we shall see, eventually recaptured Jerusalem itself.

So what do we know about the Joms-Vikings? It seems likely that they started with Harald Gormsson (otherwise known as Harald Bluetooth) marrying a Wendish Princess in 965 AD. When Harald was forced from his Scandinavian kingdom by Jarl Hakon in 985, he took refuge with the Wends and his son, Sweyn Forkbeard, formed the Joms-Vikings, initially to counter Hakon. So the first Joms-Vikings were probably mostly Wends.

The Wends were a western Slavic people, who occupied the lands of the southern Baltic, bounded by the Elbe and Saale Rivers in the West and the Oder and Neisee Rivers in the East. They were famous for their hospitality and their staunch opposition to Roman Christianity.(7)

The Joms-Vikings are mentioned in the *Jómsvíkinga Saga, King Olaf Tryggvasson's Saga* and the *Flaterjarbók*. Membership was restricted to men of proven valour between the ages of 18 to 50 (with the exception of a boy named Vagn Åkesson, who defeated Sigvaldi Strut-Haraldsson in single combat at the age of 12). To be accepted, prospective members had to prove themselves with a feat of arms in the form of a ritual duel or holmgang against another member of the Joms-Vikings.

Once admitted, the Joms-Viking was required to swear an oath and any violation was punishable by immediate expulsion from the Order. Each Joms-Viking was bound to defend his brothers, as well as avenge their deaths if necessary. It was forbidden to speak ill of his brothers or quarrel with them. Blood feuds were mediated by the Joms-Viking officers. Joms-Vikings were forbidden to show fear or flee in the face of the enemy if of equal or inferior numbers, though orderly retreat in the face of overwhelming numbers was apparently acceptable, if ordered by the officer in charge. All spoils were to be divided equally between members. No Joms-Viking was permitted to be absent from Jomsborg for more than three days without permission. No women or children were allowed within the fortress walls and none were to be captured. It is not clear if this meant that marriage or liaisons outside of the fortress were permitted.(8)

So what was the importance of the Joms-Vikings? They had been formed by Sweyn Forkbeard, son of Harald Bluetooth, both members of the Ulvungar Dynasty and descendants of Ataulf of the Visigoths and Maria of the Elchasaites and were opposed to Roman Christianity. Coincidence? Maybe, but then maybe not!

References
Chapter 6

1. Acts 22:28 & 29, KJV.
2. Acts, chap. 23.
3. Stoyanov, Y. (1994), *The Hidden Tradition in Europe*, Penguin/Arkana.
4. Martin, M. (1981), *The Decline & Fall of the Roman Church*, p. 44, G. P. Putnam's Sons, New York. See also Appendix B.
5. Stoyanov, *op. cit.* p. 88.
6. Montgomery, H. (2007), *The God-Kings of England*, App. 1, Temple Publications.
7. Army Essays (2007), The Wends 580-1218 AD, III-1a, DBA Resources.
8. Gesta Danorum (Book 10); *Jómsvíkinga saga*; *Jómsvíkingadrápa*; *Heimskringla*; *Olaf Tryggvasson's Saga*. See also Wikipedia under Jomsvikings.

Chapter 7

The Varangian Guard

The Joms-Vikings lasted until 1043, when Magnus I of Norway, a Roman Catholic Monarch, decided to put an end to them. He sacked their stronghold, Jomsborg, and put to death the remaining brethren. The Wends lasted until 1218, when they, too, were either exterminated or forced to convert to Christianity.(1)

But another elite fighting group was already making its name felt – The Varangian Guard of the Emperors of Byzantium. It is probable that the name Varangian was used for a number of Scandinavian mercenaries who were already in the pay of the Byzantine Emperors prior to 988 AD, but in 988 the Emperor Basil II requested help from Vladimir of Kiev, an Ulvungar descendant, to help him defend his throne, and in accordance with the treaty made by Vladimir's father after the siege of Dorostolon in 971.

Vladimir sent 6,000 men to Byzantium and in return was given Basil's sister, Anna, as his wife. There was however a twist to this. To marry Anna, Vladimir had to convert to Christianity, albeit of the Orthodox variety. Apparently Vladimir accepted, or at least did so in public. Basil II meanwhile led the Varangian Guards at Chrysopolis and defeated the rebel general, Bardas Phocas. Phocas apparently had a heart attack right in front of his troops and died, whereupon the rebel troops turned and fled and the Varangians happily pursued them and hacked them to pieces.

Byzantine politics were, to put it mildly, murky in the extreme and the Emperors found it difficult to trust their own native troops. The Varangians, however, were totally loyal to the person of the Emperor, though not to a particular person. For example, in 969 Emperor Nicephorus II was assassinated by his wife's lover, the Armenian General, John Tzimisces. A servant managed to raise the alarm and the Varangians rushed to the rescue. On arrival, they found that Nicephorus was dead and Tzimisces had been proclaimed Emperor. They immediately swore allegiance to the new Emperor. Had Nicephorus still been alive, they would have fought to the death for him, but once an Emperor had died and a new Emperor had been pro-claimed, then their loyalty lay with the new Emperor.(2)

Whilst it is true that the Varangians used the long axe as their main weapon, they were also proficient in all of the weapons used by the Byzantine Army and almost certainly used the Byzantine armour as opposed to the Scandinavian chain mail. We know, from the docu-mented life of Harald Hardrada, that they were proficient both on land and at sea, and had both cavalry and infantry, though it may be that they were primarily mounted infantry – in other words, they rode to battle and then dismounted to fight. There is disagreement about this amongst scholars.(3)

The Varangians lasted until at least 1209, when they were the only group to successfully defend their part of Constantinople during the 4th Crusade.(4) But a new elite fighting force was already making its presence felt – The Knights Templar.

References
Chapter 7

1. The sacking of Jomsborg is detailed in *Heimskringla*. For the Wends, see *Army Essays, op.cit.*

2. Castleden, R. (1994), *A Chronological Dictionary of Dates*, Parragon. See also *Russian Primary Chronicle*; Kekaumenos, *The Strategikon*; Komnena, Anna, *The Alexiad.*

3. McLynn, F. (1998), *1066, The Year of the Three Battles*, Chap. 3, Jonathan Cape.

4. Blondal, S. (1978), *The Varangians of Byzantium* (trans. by Benedikz, B.S.), Cambridge.

Chapter 8

The Normans and the Kingdom of Sicily

Before one can deal with the Knights Templar, it is necessary to deal with another Norman Conquest, that of Southern Italy and Sicily, because it ties in with the actual God-Kings of England, the first crusade and the eventual formation of the Knights Templar.

In some ways, the conquest of southern Italy and Sicily was one of the most impressive and certainly the most romantic of the Ulvungar conquests.(1) It is an epic tale of dusty, hard-riding warriors from northern Europe who became kings and princes in the *Sun in Oriental Splendour*.

Against them were ranged the might of the Eastern Roman Empire of Byzantium, the Western Roman Empire, the Papacy and Islam. I do not think that there was an overall plan to start with. Rather, the conquest was the result of bands of individual knights and companies of men-at-arms who were out to make their fortunes. Some, I suspect, were the remnants and later descendants of the Joms-Viking warriors. There were no kings or princes, just captains of companies made up of impoverished knights or younger sons who had no prospects at home. Though, as we shall see, the Ulvungars were heavily involved.

One such example were the Hautville brothers, who left their inadequate patrimony in Normandy "per diversa loca militariter lucrum quaerentes"(2) (seeking wealth in many places through military might). This was a "Gesta," in the traditions of the Chanson de Roland or tales of the round table. In it, we can see the ultimate exercise of aristocracy in colonisation and settlement by the imposition of Lordships, both secular and ecclesiastical, through the building of castles, churches and not least, monasteries. This may not be unique but it is peculiarly Ulvungar. We saw it in the creation of Normandy itself, in the conquest of England and we shall see it later on in this book in the creations of the Ulvungar fiefdoms in Outremer.(3)

It started in Salerno in 999 AD, before the Norman Conquest of England, but final unity was not achieved until 1130 AD, long after England was firmly under Norman control.

It started when a group of Norman knights, who were returning from Jerusalem where they had had been on pilgrimage, were staying in Salerno, when it was attacked by Saracens. The local population did not put up any resistance, having lived with these attacks for years. The knights, shocked by the non-resistance, went to see Gaimer IV, Prince of Salerno, and asked to borrow horses, arms and armour and, so equipped, proceeded to engage and drive out the infidels. So successful were they, that Gaimer asked them to stay, but they declined and returned home, laden with booty and gifts as proof of what is possible, and proceeded to recruit others.(4)

They were not the only ones recruiting. A Lombard noble from Bari, by the name of Melo, was also recruiting Normans, but he was not interested in ejecting the Saracens, he wanted recruits to eject the Byzantine rulers of Apulia.(5)

Italy at that point in time was divided into various centres of influence. Calabria (the toe of Italy) and Apulia (the heel of Italy) were part of the Byzantine Catapanate of Italy, governed from Constantinople and locally from Bari. The Papacy claimed the whole of Italy under the terms of the totally fraudulent "Donation of Constantine," though they did have a legitimate claim to Spoleto and Benevento, or most of southern Italy, by reason of a grant made by Charlemagne.

The Western Emperors, as heirs of Charlemagne, and now kings of Germany and Lombardy, claimed suzerainty over all of Lombardy and Italy. Sicily had belonged to Islam since the middle of the 9th century. Effectively the local Lombard principalities of Capua, Salerno and Benevento were virtually independent, whilst on the west coast the four duchies of Amalfi, Sorrento, Naples and Gaeta were quasi-autonomous, but attached politically to the Byzantine Catapanate. The great Benedictine Abbey and Monastery of Montecassino composed a separate principality known as "Terra Santi Benedicti."

The Normans recruited by Melo were at first extremely successful. They won a series of five victories in a row until 1018. At that point, heavily outnumbered, they met defeat at Cannae, when they came up against a powerful Byzantine Army under the Catapan Boiannes. Of the two-hundred and fifty knights who took part only ten survived, yet from this remnant there emerged a certain Rainulf "Drengot," who made himself Lord of Aversa, married the widow of the Duke of Gaeta and was eventually formally invested as Count of Aversa by the Emperor Conrad II in the summer of 1038. He was the first of the Norman "Lords" in Italy. In due course he became Duke of Gaeta, as well as Count of Aversa. Rainulf died in 1045, but his successor, Richard I, continued to build on Rainulf's success, becoming Prince of all of Capua in 1058.

Rainulf Drengot was an interesting person. He and his brothers Osmund, Gilbert (who was killed at Cannae) and Asclettin had all come south when Osmund was banished by the Duke of Normandy for killing one of his kin. The name Drengot comes from two Nordic words via Orkney – from the Hunedanic into Norman French. They are *Drengr*, meaning warrior or young man, and *Got* (from the Hunedanic Anglian *Goth*), meaning Gods (singular, *Gota*).(8) His name therefore meant "Warrior of the Gods." As we shall see later on in Fig. 6, he was related to the Ducal House. In fact, his name reminds us that, like his great-uncle, Rollo, he was a descendant of the Odonic line.

In 1035, well before the Norman Invasion of England, the first of the Hautville brothers rode into Aversa amongst the new arrivals. The brothers were William, Drogo and Humphrey, three of the twelve sons of Tancred de Hautville, by two different wives. Tancred de Hautville was a Norman Lord in the Contentin of only moderate means, so the younger sons would have to seek their fortune elsewhere rather than in Normandy. However, according to *The Complete Peerage*, Beatrice de Hautville had married Robert, Count d'Eu, grandson of Richard I of Normandy, and so the Hautvilles were related to the Ducal Family.(9)

The next part of the drama began in 1038 when the new Byzantine Emperor, Michael IV, launched a campaign against Islamic Sicily. The expedition was led by General George Maniakes, who called upon Gaimer for support. Gaimer sent three hundred of his Norman knights from Aversa, amongst them the Hautville brothers to support Maniakes. Amongst the Varangian Guard of Maniakes was a certain Harald Sigurdsson (Hardrada), who would become very important during the Invasions of England in 1066.

According to Norman sources, the expedition was not a great suc-cess. The Normans were disgusted by what they regarded as mismanagement of the campaign, though they personally distinguished themselves as capable fighters. William de Hautville unhorsed and slew the Moslem Emir of Syracuse, as a result he became known as William Bras-de-Fer, or William of the Arm of Iron.

The Normans were, however, quite happy to fight for whomever was willing to pay them and in 1041, Arduin, a rebel Lombard Lord, recruited a contingent of three hundred Normans from Aversa to fight the Byzantines. They fortified the hill town of Melfi against the Catapan. Success for the Normans came swiftly. Within days Venosa fell to them, followed by Lavello and Ascoli. That year there were three major victories against the Byzantines. The first was near Venosa on 17th March, the second at Montemaggiore on 4th May and the third at Monte Siricolo on 3rd September, when they were led by William Bras-de-Fer.

However, in 1042 Melo died and his son changed allegiance, leaving the Normans in an impossible situation. The leaders of the three main groups of Aversa, Melfi and Troia met in a grand council at Melfi, which included Rainulf I of Aversa and Gaimer, who was Prince of Capua and Salerno. The result of this council was the establishment of a series of Norman Lordships or Rulerships. William de Hautville was recognised as the leader of the Normans in Apulia and was proclaimed Count of Apulia, whilst Gaimer became Duke of Apulia, Capua and Solerno. To cement this new relationship, William married Gaimer's niece, Guida, daughter of the Duke of Sorrento.

Gaimer now divided the lands, with himself as Suzerain. Ascoli went to William de Hautville, Venoso to Drogo, whilst Siponto and Monte Gargano went to Rainulf, Count of Aversa and now Duke of Gaeta. This was eventually recognised by the Western Emperor Henry III, who confirmed Rainulf II (nephew of Rainulf I) as Count of Aversa and Drogo de Hautville as "Dux et magister Italiae comesque Normannorum totius Apuliae et Calabriae." (Duke and master in Italy and count of all the Normans in Apuliae and Calabria.) William de Hautville had died just before this.

In 1046 another Hautville arrived in Apulia, Robert, known as Guiscard (The Wary). He was the eldest son of Tancred by Tancred's second wife. With him was another knight and cousin, Richard, nephew of the reigning Count of Aversa. He is called "Richard, Asclettin's son."(6) This is interesting because it ties him into the family of the Dukes of Normandy. In my book, *The God-Kings of England*, in Appendix 2 under *Keitel's son*, I give the various names by which Rollo's father was known. Amongst them is Askettil (or Asclettin). Asclettin, it would appear, descended from Rollo's brother (see fig. 6). We can therefore conclude that Rainulf himself, as Richard's uncle, must also descend from this same family. Even more interesting is that Amatus says that Richard "rode a horse so small that his feet nearly touched the ground."(7) Was this to remind people of his collateral ancestor, Rollo, who could not find a horse large enough to ride without his feet touching the ground and hence was called "Ganger?" It seems likely. This makes the family of Rainulf not only a branch of the great Ulvungar dynasty, but cousins to the ruling house of Normandy and they were cousins to the Hautvilles, who were also related to the Ducal House (see Appendix G, House of Grantmesnil). Judith, the daughter of William, Count of Evreux, and grand-daughter of Robert I of Normandy married Robert de Hautville, Count of Sicily. Her cousin, Arnold de Grantmesnil, went to Apulia with the Hautvilles.

Osmund, one of Asclettin's sons (see fig. 6), had killed a member of the Ducal Family, but because he was himself a cousin, the Duke had him sent into exile in Italy instead of hanging him on the spot.

Fig. 6

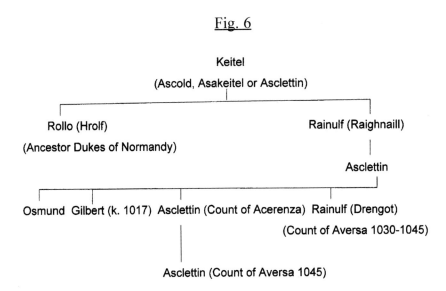

(There may be a generation missing between Rainulf [Raighnaill] and Asclettin.) For a list of the Norman Counts of Aversa and Princes of Capua see Appendix H.

In 1047 Robert de Hautville was sent south to try his luck against Byzantine Calabria. He established himself at San Marco Argentano, where he met and married Alberada, who brought with her a dowry of two hundred knights. With these forces he was able to conquer the surrounding area.

All these successes were making the Normans very unpopular with certain important people, notably the Byzantine Emperor and the Pope, who now combined forces against the Normans. On 18th June 1053, near the town of Civitate, the Normans attacked the Papal forces and routed them completely. Humphrey held the centre, Richard of Aversa the right wing and Robert Guiscard led the left wing. The Suabian elite guard with their two-handed swords went down in defeat, just as in 1066 the Saxons, wielding their battle-axes, went down in defeat at Hastings.

The Normans were there to stay. Now began the final part of the conquest, the Invasion of Sicily itself. The Invasion of Sicily began in 1061, five years before the Invasion of England. The crossing was made from Santa Maria del Foro, at night, with the landfall just south of Messina. It was made by two hundred and seventy knights and their horses on thirteen ships. Having established a bridgehead, a further one hundred and seventy followed and with this force, Robert took the city of Messina.

When the main Army arrived they quickly took Rometta and Paterno. The Norman forces, which probably only numbered some 700 mounted knights, defeated a Saracen Army of 15,000 but the mountain fortress of Enna was impregnable. With the heat of summer and limited resources, further campaigning was halted.

The campaign on Sicily itself, from this point on, became the work of Roger de Hautville. He eventually took Palermo in 1072, eleven years after the invasion began. Roger was made Count of Sicily and, at this point, the end for Sicily was never in doubt, although it would be another twenty years before Noto finally fell. Trapani was captured in 1077, Taormina in 1079, Syracuse in 1085 and the impregnable fortress of Enna in 1087.

1091 marks the final conquest of Sicily, some thirty years in all, and marking the beginning of the fabulous Kingdom of the Two Sicilies. The kings of the Two Sicilies would reign in Oriental splendour from their Capital in Palermo for some three hundred years. For a time, they ruled not only over the two Sicilies, but large chunks of North Africa. Yet in 1098 the Ulvungars started the greatest of all their conquests. The first crusade was about to begin.

Notes and References:
Chapter 8

There are an enormous amount of sources for the Norman doings in Italy: Ordericus Vitalis – *Ecclesiastical History*; Matus of Montecassino – *Storia de' Normanni*; Gaufridus Malaterra – *Historia Sicula*; to name but a few, as well as Islamic, Byzantine and other sources. Then, too, there are numerous articles and books by such luminaries as J. J. Norwich, Prof. R. Allen Brown, Dr. Loud of Nottingham University and others. However, this chapter was written entirely from my lecture notes for talks I gave at the Megatrend University of Applied Sciences in Belgrade and subsequently, to the History courses at the Uttoxeter and Stafford U3As. During my researches for these lectures, I consulted most of these sources or authorities but cannot remember, in all cases, which particular source I used for which part. I apologise to my readers for this lapse and hope they will forgive the memory of an old man.

1. R. Allen Brown (1984), *The Normans*, p. 93, Boydell Press.
2. Malaterra, Gaufridus (c. 1098), Historia Sicula, ed. Migne, Patrologia Latina.
3. Montgomery, H., *The God-Kings of England, op. cit.* Chap. VII.
4. Montgomery, H. (2004), *The Normans in the South*, Lectures in Medieval History, University of the 3rd Age.
5. Ibid.
6. Amatus of Montecassino, *Storia de' Normanni*, ed. Bartholomaeis, p. 110; trans. Norwich, J. J.
7. Ibid.
8. Montgomery, Count B. G. (1968) *Ancient Migrations and Royal Houses*, p. 166, The Mitre Press, London.
9. *The Complete Peerage*, vol. V, pp.152-153.

Chapter 9

The First Crusade and the Establishment of Outremer

I am going to divide this chapter into three parts: the establishment of the Principality of Antioch, the establishment of the County of Edessa and finally, the establishment of the Kingdom of Jerusalem.

The seminal work on the Crusades is undoubtedly that of Sir Steven Runciman, (1) and I shall be using this work as a basis for most of this chapter, though quoting directly from sources where appropriate.

On 27th November 1095, at a meeting in Clermont, France, Pope Urban II made a plea for Christians to "take the cross" and to liberate the East, the Eastern Churches and the Holy Places from the *Infidel*. This speech launched the First Crusade. However, Pope Urban had taken some precautions that his address would receive a warm welcome. Urban had journeyed to Clermont via Avignon and St. Gilles, where he had consulted with Adhemar, Bishop of Le Puy, and Raymond IV of St. Gilles, Count of Toulouse and Marquis of Provence (and married to the Princess Elvira of Aragon). These two had given him their backing in advance and were the first to take the cross. Their example fired the imagination of others, including lords, clerics and ordinary laity.

I do not think that Urban expected quite the overwhelming reaction he got and, particularly, the effect on the illiterate laity who formed the "People's Crusade," led by the fanatical Peter the Hermit. Peter never reached Palestine, but was cut to pieces by the Turks at Civetot in Asia Minor, miles away from Jerusalem and the Holy Land. Those not slaughtered were sold into slavery. Other disorganised groups from, for example, Germany, only reached Hungary, where they proceeded to slaughter Jews and were themselves wiped out by the local populace in retaliation for their atrocities.(2)

The real Crusaders took their time and organised themselves properly. The first of these was Raymond IV of St. Gilles. He had been a veteran of the wars against the Muslims in Spain and, more than anybody, knew what the Crusaders were likely to face. He was, at this point, about 60 years old and decided to leave his great possessions in France and stay, for the rest of his life, in Outremer. He took with him his wife, Elvira, and his infant son, Alfonso. With him went many of the great nobles of Southern France, including Count Rambald of Orange and William Bishop of Orange, Gaston de Béarn, Gerard de Roussillon and William of Montpellier.(3) Raymond's forces numbered about ten thousand, of which about one thousand two hundred were Knights and Cavalry, and the remainder infantry.(4) Raymond's forces set out in October, 1096.

The next great magnate was Hugh de Vermandois, younger son of King Henry I of France. His was one of the smallest groups, only about one hundred Knights, but they were the first to actually get underway, leaving France in August of 1096.

From Normandy came Robert, Duke of Normandy, eldest son of William the Conqueror, who had mortgaged his lands to his brother, William II, King of England, in order to equip his forces. He was joined by Stephan-Henri, Count of Blois, who had married Adele, William the Conqueror's daughter and Robert's sister. With them went Robert, Count of Flanders, their first cousin. This combined force numbered some two thousand two hundred knights and about eight thousand infantry.(5)

Amongst the Anglo-Norman and Breton lords who accompanied these three were Alan Fergant, Count of Brittany; Stephan Count of Aumale; Odo, Bishop of Bayeaux, the Conqueror's half-brother; Ralph de Gael (or Gauder), titular Earl of Norfolk; Pain Peveral, the Duke's standard bearer; Philip de Montgomery, Lord of the Manor of Wenlock in Shropshire, who was killed at the taking of Jerusalem; his eldest brother, Robert de Bellême, and William de Percy.(6)

This contingent travelled south into Italy and down into what was becoming Norman Southern Italy.(7) Duke Robert Curthose overwintered with Roger Borsa, Guiscard's son and heir and now Duke of Apulia, Calabria and Sicily, and eventually took ship from Brindisi in the spring of 1097. As a consequence, he was the last of the great crusading Magnates to arrive in Constantinople.(8)

There was also another Norman contingent, that of the Normans of the South (Italy), under Bohemond of Taranto. Bohemond was the eldest son of Guiscard by his first wife, Aubrey, but had been disinherited upon Guiscard divorcing Aubrey and remarrying for political gain. This group was small, only about five hundred knights, but they easily made up for their small numbers in expertise and knowledge in fighting the Saracens. These knights included most of the leading nobles and knights of Norman Italy, including the ruling houses of Capua and Apulia. The Hautvilles were strongly represented, not only by Bohemond himself, but by his nephew Tancred, his cousins Richard of the Principate, Herman of Canne, Robert, son of Girard, who acted as Bohemond's standard bearer, and Geoffrey of Montescaglioso. Another nephew, William, had gone ahead to accompany Hugh de Vermandois.(9)

From Lorraine came Godfrey de Bouillon, Duke of Lower Lorraine, with his brothers Eustace, Count of Boulogne, and Baldwin, his cousin Baldwin of Le Bourg, another Baldwin, Count of Hainult, and Rainald, Count of Toul. They rode through Germany and Hungary and arrived on 23rd December 1096 in Constantinople.

It is worthwhile, at this point, to look at the ancestry of these nobles. Let us start with Raymond of Toulouse or St. Gilles (1042-1105). He was the son of Pons of Toulouse and Almodis de la Marche. Another Almodis de la Marche , niece of the first, married Roger de Poictiers, Earl of Lancaster, third son of Roger de Montgomery, one of the main Ulvungar families and fourth cousin to Robert, Duke of Normandy. This Almodis was Countess de le Marche in her own right, her father having no male heirs and their descendants became Counts de la Marche, dropping their ancestral name, Montgomery.(10) Raymond was followed as Count of Toulouse by Bertrand, who married Aliza, daughter of Eudo, Duke of Burgundy, and upon his death she married William de Montgomery, Prince of Bellême, Count of Ponthieu and

Alençon and grandson of Roger de Montgomery. They had several children including Ela, who married William, Earl of Warren and Surrey, Guy, who became Count of Ponthieu and Prince of Bellême, and Jean de Montgomery (died 24th February 1190), Count of Alençon, who became Grand Chamberlain to the kings of Jerusalem and supervised the Temple Mount. Another son, Robert de Montgomery, went to Scotland in the train of David I and married Margery, daughter of Walter the High Steward, progenitor of the Royal Family of Steward (Stuart). The last child, a daughter Giles, married the Laird of MacIntosh and whose descendants became not only Chief of Clan MacIntosh, but later, Chiefs of Clan Chattan, the Clan of the Cats.(11)

One can immediately see the careful marriages that were taking place – The Plaited Cord – as I call it, between these great Ulvungar families.

It is also noteworthy in that, according to Armenian sources, Raymond IV lost an eye before the First Crusade and was called "Monoculos," or "one-eyed," a bit like Odin! It is probable that he lost this eye in a fight against the Moors, whom he had fought before going on Crusade. In fact, he married three times and was twice excommunicated by the Pope for marrying within the forbidden degrees of consanguinity. His first wife was his first cousin and mother of Bertrand, his heir; his second wife was Matilda, daughter of King Roger I of Sicily and his third was Elvira, illegitimate daughter of King Alfonso VI of Castile. He took his infant son by Elvira and Elvira herself with him on Crusade. The infant would die on the way.(12) The list of the Counts of Toulouse is given in Appendix (R).

The second of these magnates was Hugh, Count of Vermandois, known as Hugh the Great. He descended from Pepin I, Count of Vermandois (886-892) and son of the Carolingian Bernard, King of Italy. Hugh was the son of Henry I of France and Anne of Kiev (an Ulvungar). He was therefore descended from the Davidic Carolingian line, as well as the Odonic/Davidic line.

Robert of Normandy was, of course, Ulvungar to his finger tips, being a descendant of Rollo, Bjorn Ironside and Ragnar Lothbroc. Most of his senior nobles were also family: Stephan-Henri of Blois, married to Robert's sister; Robert of Flanders, his first cousin; Fergant of Brittany, another cousin; Odo of Bayeaux, his uncle; and Robert de Bellême, eldest son of Roger de Montgomery; his brother, Philip de Montgomery; and the heir of Mortagne, yet another cousin. Just as the successful invasion of England had been organised and executed by the Ulvungar cousins, so now the First Crusade would be as well.(13)

The Norman-Italian contingent's background has already been dealt with in the previous chapter. Suffice it to say there were many Ulvungars in their ranks.

Approximately a fortnight after arriving at Constantinople the armies of the west embarked for Palestine. The first place to which the crusading armies laid siege was Nicaea, which has always struck me as the place that they should start, being the place of the famous Council in 325 AD. The attack was planned for 19th of June, but on the very morning of the attack, the Crusaders awoke to find the flag of the Byzantine Emperor flying from the citadel. The Turks had surrendered the city during the night and, as the inhabitants were mostly Christian, the Emperor had no wish for the city to have to withstand siege and sack. It had always been part of the Imperial domain and it was now back firmly under imperial control.

Anna Comnena, the daughter of the Emperor, admits that the Emperor tricked the Crusaders, but each soldier was given a considerable amount of gold and silver to compensate them. Stephen of Blois was amazed by the amount of gold and jewels that fell to him, though some were not so happy.(14)

The Emperor allowed the Turkish court officials and commanders to buy their freedom and the Sultana, the daughter of Emir Chaka, was received with royal honours. She and her children were then sent to her husband, free of ransom. This was not to the liking of some of the Crusaders, but the Emperor well knew the advantage of kindness and putting the Emir in his debt.(15)

On 26th June the Crusaders left Nicaea and moved off towards the bridge over the Blue River. There they halted whilst the leaders took counsel. The problem was that they had to cross a desert in which there was no water and could only be crossed by contingents moving fairly fast, which the army was not able to do as a group. It was therefore decided to divide the army into two groups, the first to precede the second by a day.

In the vanguard were the Normans, both those from southern Italy and those from Normandy itself, and their allies. With them went the Byzantine contingent, who were acting as guides. The leader of the first group was Bohemond. The second group were the Lorrainers, French and Vermandois under the overall command of Raymond of Toulouse.

On 30th June the crusading army encamped in the plain not far from Dorylaeum, but the Sultan, Kilij Arslan, together with the Danishmend Emir and his vassal Hasan, Emir of Cappadocia, were waiting for them. At sunrise the Turkish army attacked, swooping down from the hillside. Bohemond was not unprepared, however. Non-combatants and women were assembled in the centre, where there were springs of water, and the women were given the task of taking water to the forward troops. A messenger was sent galloping off to the second crusader contingent, asking them to hurry. Bohemond then told his knights to dismount and, for the time being, to keep on the defensive. Only one of knights disobeyed who, with forty of his men, charged the enemy but retreated, covered in wounds.

The Turks carried out their favourite tactic of showering the defenders with arrows from a series of movements, whereby each group galloped forward, discharged their arrows and then made way for a new group. As the morning advanced, with the sun beating down, the first group of crusaders began to wonder if they could hold out from these attacks. As any surrender would mean death or slavery, and as many of the women were wives of the nobles and knights, they decided that they would hold out to the last and, if necessary, kill their own wives rather than allow them to be captured.

At about noon they saw the second crusader group arrive with Godfrey and Hugh in the lead, and Raymond and his group close behind. The Turks had not realised that they had not entrapped the whole of the crusading army and started to falter. The two groups were able to join and the defenders now mounted their horses. Forming a long front with Bohemond, Robert of Normandy and Stephen of Blois on the left, Raymond and Robert of Flanders in the centre, and Godfrey and Hugh on the right, they charged the Turks. Before they charged they were told: "Stand fast all together, trusting in Christ and in the victory of the Holy Cross. Today please God we shall all gain much booty." Holy enterprise it may have been, but the last phrase says it all, this was a group of warriors seeking booty just as their Viking ancestors had done.(16)

The Turks were unprepared for an attack and were probably running short of arrows when, to their horror, yet another army appeared on the hills behind them, thus totally hemming them in. This group was led by the Bishop Adhemar of Le Puy, who had planned this himself and found guides to bring him through the mountain passes. His intervention caused the Turks to panic and take flight towards the East, leaving their encampment intact. The tents of the Sultan and the two Emirs fell together with all their treasure to the Crusaders.

It was a great victory, but many Crusaders lost their lives, including Tancred's brother, William. The Europeans had also learned to respect the Turkish warriors. The crusading army now rested for two days at Dorylaeum to recover and plan their next stage. I do not intend in this book to go over the ground covered so eloquently by Sir Steven Runciman. The problems of heat, crossing a desert without water and the difficulties of the pass known as the Syrian Gates are all recounted by him. My purpose in this book is to show what the families and members of the Ulvungar dynasty did.

On 10th September the army split. Tancred, with the Normans of southern Italy, Godfrey's brother Baldwin, and some of his followers set off for the Taurus pass, whilst the main army headed for Caesarea. At the end of the month, after a minor battle with the Emir Hasan, the main body reached Caesarea. Tancred, meanwhile, took Tarsus, the capital of Cilicia, but was forced to give it up to Baldwin, whose contingent was bigger than Tancred's. One should note the help given by the Bagratide family, the princely family of Armenia and adherents of the Armenian, as opposed to Orthodox, Christian Church.(17)

Tancred moved on to Adana, whilst up the river to Tarsus sailed Guynemer. He was a professional pirate or Viking, and realised that the Crusaders would need naval help to keep them supplied. He collected a group of Danes, Frisians and Flemings, sailed from the Netherlands and made contact with Baldwin in Tarsus. In part, because Baldwin was the brother of his Count, he made homage to Baldwin, who promptly borrowed three hundred men to garrison Tarsus and nominated Guynemer as his lieutenant, so that he, Baldwin, could move on.

Meanwhile, the main army made for Antioch, which they had to take in order to enter Palestine proper. The city of Antioch covered an area of about three miles long and about a mile deep, between the River Orontes and Mount Silpius. In place were huge fortifications that had been constructed by Justinian and repaired a century earlier by Byzantine artisans, using their most up-to-date technology. To the north the walls arose from marshy ground and to the east and west they climbed up a steep mountainside, ending along the summit of the ridge and culminating in a superb citadel a thousand feet above the town. Four hundred towers rose from this citadel, spaced so that every one was in bowshot of the next. A whole army could be housed in the town and provisioned against a long siege. It would be impossible for the Crusaders to take it by assault. There was no way they could even surround it. It was only through treachery that the Turks had taken it in 1085.(18)

The resident governor was Yaghi-Siyan and the one thing he dreaded was treachery, being himself an expert at it.(19) On 20th October the army reached the Orontes by the Iron Bridge. The bridge was heavily fortified with towers flanking the entrance, but the soldierly Bishop of Le Puy directed operations and the Crusaders attacked at once, forcing their way across. In so doing, they were able to capture a huge convey of provisions of sheep, cattle and corn intended for the city. This not only helped the crusaders, but denied the food to Yaghi-Sivan's troops.

On their arrival the Crusaders set up their tents outside the northeast side of the walls. Bohemond took the sector near to the St. Paul Gate, Raymond the position opposite the Gate of the Dog, and Godfrey opposite the Gate of the Duke. The rest of the army waited behind Bohemond to be directed to wherever they might be needed. For the time being, the Crusaders left the Bridge Gate and the Gate of St. George unattended.

Yaghi-Sivan had expected an immediate assault and when this did not happen, suspected the worst. Many of the people in the city were Christian and this caused Yaghi-Sivan to become very nervous.

Raymond indeed suggested assault, but the remaining leaders were a little more circumspect. Their troops were tired and they could not afford great losses at this point. Furthermore, reinforcements were expected from Tancred in Alexandria and they hoped that Guynemer's fleet might aid them. They also needed the Emperor to supply them with siege engines.

Between then and June of the following year there were a considerable number of skirmishes and even major battles as the Crusaders overcame forces sent to relieve the city. Not all were won by the Crusaders. Many perished from hunger and thirst and most of the horses were lost. Eventually, however, the city was taken by treachery just as Yaghi-Sivan had dreaded. He, himself, was thrown from his horse trying to escape and was killed by local Christians, who cut off his head and sent it to Bohemond. It was Bohemond who had made the initial contact with a captain called Firouz, a Christian convert to Islam, who eventually handed the Crusaders an entrance to the city. By nightfall on 3rd June 1098, not one Turk was left alive in Antioch. In the confusion, many Christians were killed and the houses of all, whether Muslim or Christian, were pillaged. "You could not walk on the streets without treading on corpses, all of them rotting rapidly in the summer heat."(20)

Hardly had they taken over when they, themselves, were besieged by the Atabeg Kerbogha, who now arrived with an enormous host. The Crusaders now found themselves in the same position as Yaghi-Sivan. They had expected help from the Emperor, but Alexius, on poor advice, had turned back with the Imperial Army, leaving the Crusaders to fend for themselves. This, more than anything else, caused the Crusaders to refuse to hand over their conquests to the Emperor, which they had all taken an oath to do.

Eventually, thanks to the generalship of Bohemond, the intervention of the Holy Lance, supposedly discovered by Peter Bartholemew, and the desertions of many of Kerbogha's Emirs, the Crusaders fought and put to flight the Turkish Army. They established Antioch as a Christian City, which was, after some hesitation, handed over to Bohemond as his fief.

Let us now return to Baldwin, who had left the main army at Marash. At first, Baldwin took a parallel road to the north so as to protect the main force from raids from that direction, however at Ain-tab, Baldwin turned sharply to the East. There is considerable difference of opinion as to why he did this, but in part it was at the suggestion of Bagrat, brother of Kogh Vasil and a Prince of Armenia. Kogh Vasil's lordship lay to the east of Marash, whilst Thoros of Edessa sent an urgent message to Baldwin appealing for help. The Armenians had always looked to the West to help them, as they wanted independence from both the Turks, on the one hand, and the Emperor on the other. They therefore looked upon the Baldwin as a liberator.(21)

It seems we never learn from history. Today, in Iraq and Afghanistan, they are learning the lessons of "liberation" all over again, just as the Armenians did a thousand years ago. During the winter of 1097 Baldwin completed his conquest of the area up to the Euphrates, taking the only two fortresses – Ruwandan and Tel-Bashir – which Baldwin renamed Ravendel and Turbessel. Ravendel, which was his communication point with Antioch, was put under the governorship of Bagrat. Another Armenian, Fer, was put in charge of Turbessel, which commanded an important ford across the Euphrates.

Whilst at Turbessel, Baldwin received an embassy from Thoros of Edessa asking him to hurry and come to Edessa. Thoros's position was difficult. He had heard that the terrible Atabeg Kerbogha, Emir of Mosul was gathering an army to relieve Antioch, but Kerbogha's route would take him through Armenian territory and, in particular, past Edessa. Thoros, who was childless and aging, offered to adopt Baldwin as his son and make him co-ruler of his domains. This situation worried Bagrat, who consulted his brother Kogh Vasil. It seems likely that Baldwin was led to believe that Bagrat was fomenting rebellion, because he sent troops to Ravendel and had Bagrat arrested and tortured. Bagrat escaped, went to join his brother, and the two became guerrillas in the mountains.(22)

In February 1098, Baldwin left Tubessel with about eighty knights and headed for Edessa, arriving there on the 6th of February. He was received with great rejoicing, both by Thoros and the population as a whole. Almost immediately, Thoros formally adopted Baldwin as his son and made him co-regent of Edessa. Baldwin then led a combined expedition against the Turkish Emir of Samosata. The Edessene troops turned out to be pretty poor. They were ambushed and a large number killed, but Bladwin was able to capture a fortified village called St. John, close to the Emir's capital and, by placing most of his knights there, was able to stop the Emir from raiding the Edessene's lands. In this he was helped by an Armenian Princeling called Constantine of Gargar. On their return, Constantine evolved a plot to replace Thoros with Baldwin. Although Thoros had, throughout his life, managed to keep Edessa more or less independent, his people were not particularly grateful to him and it seemed they hated him, probably because of high taxes and his inability to protect them and their livestock from raids.

It seemed to them that Baldwin had achieved the latter within weeks. On Thursday, March 3rd, Thoros was overthrown. Thoros attempted to escape but was captured and torn to pieces by the crowd. On Wednesday, March 10th, Baldwin was asked to accept the rulership.

Baldwin took the title Count of Edessa, a surprisingly humble title, but in theory he was still under oath to the Emperor Alexius. He was enabled shortly afterwards to achieve a real political and diplomatic triumph. He had discovered in the treasury a vast store of treasure, some dating from Byzantine days and some from Thoros's taxes, and with this he was able to purchase the Emirate of Samosata from the Turkish Emir Balduk who, frightened of Baldwin's new reign, offered to sell his Emirate for ten thousand bezants. He also took over the famous Royal Library of Edessa, said to contain letters between Jesus and the First Century King of Edessa.(23)

Baldwin accepted and entered Samosata in triumph. There he found a number of prisoners from Edessa that Balduk had captured, whom he promptly freed and returned to their families. Balduk and his body-guard were invited to take up residence in Edessa as mercenaries of Baldwin's. Later Balduk was to rebel and was beheaded.

Baldwin set out clear principles for the governance of his county. The control of government was in the hands of Franks, but Orientals, both Muslim and Christian, were encouraged to take part in the State. This eventually created a fusion that, had it lasted longer, would have seen the county become a template for the Latin States of Outremer, just as the Southern Normans were to do in Italy. Thus was born the second of the great fiefs of Outremer.

Within a year, Baldwin, now a widower, had married the daughter of a local Armenian Prince, Taphnuz, and had captured Saruj and Birejik, thus consolidating his county and enabling him to communi-cate directly with the rest of the Crusade. He had countered a rebellion by local Armenians and had attracted large numbers of Western European knights to his standard. Furthermore, when Kerbogha laid siege to Edessa for three weeks, not only was Kerbogha unsuccessful, but his delay saved the main Crusade. Baldwin's star was rising fast. He had started the Crusade as a youngest son dependent upon his brothers' bounty. Now he was more powerful and a lot richer than they, themselves.

Let us now return to the main Crusade. The last of the great Fortresses that had to be taken and the raison d'etre of the Crusade was the City of Jerusalem, a city holy to Jews, Muslims and Christians alike.

It is not the place of this book to deal with the journey from Antioch to Jerusalem; it is dealt with in detail in Chapter 10 of Runciman's *History of the Crusades*.(24) Suffice it to say that the Crusaders delayed moving out from Antioch for fifteen months, and when they did move out there was considerable disagreement between the leaders as to who should be in charge. Raymond of Toulouse asserted his rights, but these were challenged by both Robert of Flanders and Robert of Normandy. The Crusaders eventually reached the Walls of Jerusalem on Tuesday, 7th June 1099.

Just over a month later, on the 13th and 14th July, and after at least one abortive attempt to scale the walls, the Crusaders stormed the walls. They had been aided by the arrival of several ships in the port of Jaffa, which brought with them much needed nails, cordage and materials to construct siege towers. It was these which, suddenly appearing and being placed against the walls, enabled the Crusaders to take first one wall and then the entire city. All Christians had already left the city on the orders of the Fatimid governor, Iftikhar ad-Dawla, as soon as the Crusaders had arrived, so the only inhabitants were Muslims or Jews. They were all slaughtered, men, women and children, the Jews being burnt to death in their own synagogue. This bloodbath has echoed down through the centuries. This bloodthirsty Christian fanaticism has produced Muslim fanaticism in its wake. Later, when wiser men sought to find a way in which the various religions could live together, this massacre has always stood in the way.

When no more Muslims were left to slay, the Crusaders went in procession to the Church of the Holy Sepulchre to give thanks, then, on 17th July, the princes all met to decide who should rule in Jerusalem.

According to Runciman, had Bishop Adhemar of Le Puy still been alive, it is probable that he would have been offered the roll of Prince-Bishop of Jerusalem, but Adhemar had died on 1st August of the previous year in Antioch. Furthermore, Pope Urban, who had planned or at least preached the Crusade, died on 29th July 1099, before news of the success of the Crusade could reach him. There was no Papal authority until a new Pope was elected and in addition, Rome was too far away.

There is considerable difference of opinion among scholars as to whom the Crown of Jerusalem was first offered. According to Raymond of Aguilers, Raymond of Toulouse was first offered the crown but refused.(25) According to Odericus Vitalis, it was offered first to Robert of Normandy.(26)

Let us examine these two claims in detail. One needs, first of all, to look at who were to select the Ruler. The clergy suggested that, first and foremost, a spiritual leader should be appointed. This was rejected by the leaders. William of Tyre, though admittedly writing almost a hundred year later, was scandalised by this attitude of the Church to go beyond its remit, even though he himself was a Bishop.

We do not know with certainty who formed the college of electors, but it is probable that the senior clergy, the princes and their tenants-in-chief formed it. If the crown was first offered to Raymond, why did he refuse it?

He had always maintained that he was going to end his days in Palestine, at the time he took the cross. He had striven to become the leader of the Crusade. When he did take command, he showed himself to have a poor grasp of what was required against the Turks, and his military attempts had generally ended in disaster unless he was rescued by Bohemond. The account by Raymond of Aguilers that Raymond had been offered the crown, but had replied that he would not "wear a crown in the city where Jesus had worn one of thorns" is factually incorrect. This was said by the clergy to stop the appointment of a temporal, as opposed to a spiritual, ruler of Jerusalem. When it was eventually offered to Godfrey, Raymond sulked and announced that if anyone except himself was to wear the crown, he would leave Jerusalem. He eventually set himself up in Jericho.(27) If he wanted the crown, why refuse it when offered? It does not make a lot of sense, unless he was trying a "Caesar" and wanted it to be offered to him three times before accepting! I have my doubts about it being offered to Raymond at all.

Let us now look at Robert of Normandy. In *The God-Kings of England*, I have shown that the Norman Dukes undoubtedly knew from whom they were descended.(28) They almost certainly had in their possession the Latin document I have shown in the text, known as *The House of Bethany Document*. They knew, too, their Davidic background. Dudo of Saint Quentin had been shown a document, probably this one, when writing his *History of the Ducal House*, which had terrified and amazed him.(29) I believe it may well have been the Latin document that I have shown as Fig. 2. When William the Conqueror built the White Tower, which eventually became the Tower of London, he flattened every building within bowshot of his tower. Yet he allowed a Jewish ritual bath to be built within less than a mile from the tower. It would have stuck out like a sore thumb! Nobody could have built it without William's personal permission. He must, therefore, have been very sure that the people who would use it were family related.

If, therefore, the Ducal family knew their own ancestry it seems to me to be likely that other royal and noble families would also know this, and if he was judged by them to be the most senior of the Davidic line, it seems to me logical that he would have been offered the Crown of Jerusalem. But if this whole Crusade had been only to restore the Davidic line to Jerusalem why then, did Robert refuse it? We are faced with the same problem, unless of course there was a crown that he wanted more than that of Jerusalem? How about the Crown of England!

He was the eldest son of William the Conqueror and it was likely that William may well have indicated that Robert should become not only Duke of Normandy, but also King of England. It was only when Robert rebelled against his own father that William decided to make his second son, William, his heir to England.

Let us look at the facts:

1. Robert had mortgaged his Duchy to William to fund the Crusade. But if William were to die, then the mortgage would be null and void. In those days, they were personal to the individual.

2. Robert refuses the Crown of Jerusalem and heads for home in December, 1099.

3. 2nd August 1100, William II, King of England, is killed by an arrow whilst out hunting. Sir Walter Tyrel, who fired the arrow, flees England and goes to his estates in Ponthieu, within the Duchy of Normandy. It is, in fact, in the county of which Robert de Montgomery/Bellême happens to be Count, having married Agnes, only daughter and heir of Ponthieu, and who just happens to be in the direct line of descent from Charlemagne (30), but Duke Robert is still on his way back to Normandy.

4. Henry, who is in England, usurps the crown whilst Robert is still on his way home, and has himself crowned as Henry I. Did Henry engineer his brother's death before Robert could return – and who would then have a better claim?

5. Robert arrives back in Normandy and promptly invades England to claim his right to the throne.

It seems to me, therefore, that if the Crown of Jerusalem had been offered to Robert of Normandy, he may well have refused it and passed it on to the next in line in both the Davidic and Charlemagnic succession – Godfrey of Bouillon who, interestingly enough, does not take the title of King of Jerusalem but "Guardian or Defender of the Holy Sepulchre," precisely the same title that Charlemagne received prior to becoming Roman Emperor.(31)

His enjoyment of the title was not to last. On 18th July 1100, Godfrey, Duke of Bouillon, Guardian of the Holy Sepulchre, died. His brother, Baldwin, Count of Edessa, was his heir, but he did not hear of his brother's death until August and did not enter Jerusalem until 9th November. On 11th November 1100, Baldwin accepted the title "King of Jerusalem" and on Christmas Day, 1100, was formally consecrated by the Patriarch Daimbert, just as William I had been crowned King of England on Christmas Day, 1066. Why Christmas Day? Because this was supposedly the birthday of Jesus and they were proclaiming to the world that they were his descendants. So Baldwin, the youngest, penniless son of Eustace of Boulogne, but descendant of the Davidic/Odonic line, became the first King of Jerusalem since Herod. The Ulvungars were back in the city of their ancestors and this time they were kings.

They had fought and captured that which was lost.

But finally, betrayal would cost them the city.

References
Chapter 9

1. Runciman, Sir S. (1951), *The History of the Crusades*, Vols. I, II & III, Cambridge University Press.
2. *Ibid* pp. 124-141.
3. Brown, R.A. (1984), *The Normans*, p. 132, Boydell Press.
4. Runciman, *op. cit.* Appendix II.
5. David, C. W. (1920), *Robert Curthose*, Appendix D, Harvard University Press.
6. *Ibid.* See also Montgomery, H. (2002), *Montgomery Millennium*, p. 1-3, Megatrend, Belgrade & London.
7. See previous chapter.
8. Brown, *op.cit.* p. 133.
9. *Ibid.*
10. Montgomery, *op. cit.* p. 3. There is a stained glass window in the parish church in Lancaster of Roger de Poictiers carrying a shield with a lion rampant and gold bordure. The window, from a later time, shows a later concept in heraldry. It is doubtful that Roger ever had a shield painted with this device, but he would certainly have had a banner, which may well have been painted in this way. A copy of the window is shown on page II-3 of the cited book.
11. Montgomery, *op. cit.* pp. 1-3. Also Bain, R. (1938), *The Clans and Tartans of Scotland* (7th Edition), p. 194, W. Collins & Sons.
12. Raymond of Aguilers (c. 1100), *Historia Francorum qui ceperunt Jerusalem*, R.H.C. Occ. Vol. III. Also Runciman, *op. cit.* pp. 106-340. Also Payne, R. (1984), *The Dream & the Tomb*. Also Encyclopaedia Britannica, 11th Edition. Also
http://fmg.ac/Projects/MedLands/TOULOUSE.htm#_Toc149811414.
13. Montgomery, H. (2007), *The God-Kings of England*, Temple Publications. Also Runciman, *op. cit.* p.165.
14. Comnena, A. (c. 1100), *Alexiad* (ed. B. Leib) xi, 4-6, vol. III, pp 12-13, Collection Byzantine de l'Association Guilaume Budé, Paris (1937- 1945).
15. Runciman, *op cit.* vol. I. p. 182.
16. Rosalind Hill (ed.) (1962), *Gesta Francorum*, pp.19-20, Nelson Medieval Texts, London.
17. Runciman, *op. cit.* p. 197.

18. William of Tyre, Historia (c. 1200), *Rerum in Partibus Transmarinis Gestarum* (In R.H.C. Occ. IV, 9-10, I 165-169). Also quoted by Runciman, ibid.

19. Runciman, *op.cit.* pp. 213-216.

20. Runciman, *Ibid*, p. 235.

21. Runciman, *Ibid*, pp. 200-203.

22. Albert of Aix, (c.1100) - *Liber Christianae Expeditionis pro Ereptione, Emundatione et Restitutione Sanctae Hierosolymitanae Ecclesiae*, III, 18, p. 351.

23. *Abdias Manuscript*, p. 102b, Norris Collection and in the possession of the author.

24. Runciman, *op. cit.* Chapter 10.

25. Raymond of Aguilers, *op. cit.* XX, p. 301.

26. Ordericus Vitalis, *Historia Ecclesiastica.*

27. Raymond of Aguilers, *op. cit.* XX, pp. 301-302, and William of Tyre, *op. cit.* IX3, vol. I, pp. 367-368.

28. Montgomery, *op. cit.* p.116.

29. *Ibid.*

30. *Ibid*, App. XIII.

31. Zuckerman, A. J. (1972), *A Jewish Princedom in Feudal France768-900,* pp. 186-191, Columbia University Press, New York & London. Also, Montgomery, H. *The God-Kings of Europe, op. cit.* p. 75.

Chapter 10

The Kingdom of Jerusalem and the Formation of the Knights Templar

It seems to be generally agreed on various Internet sites that the founders of the Knights Templar were as follows: Hugh de Payen, André de Montbard, Godfrey or Geoffroi of St. Omer, Payen de Montdidier, Achambaud de St. Amand, Geoffroi Bisol or Bisot, Gondemare or Gondamar, Rosal or Roland, and Godfroi. However William of Tyre, writing one hundred years later, mentions only two names – Hughes de Payen and André de Montbard.(1) The other names, so far as I can gather, appear as early members of the Templars, but otherwise are unknown.

Let us look at what, if anything, is known about each and see what the likelihood is that they formed the Order of Knights Templar and why. Hugh de Payen is undoubtedly the best known. He was supposedly a vassal of Hugh de Champagne and seems to have gone out with the main crusading army in 1096. As a vassal of Champagne he would almost certainly have gone out under the leadership of Hugh de Vermandois, who is known to have taken several knights from Champagne with him. However, his name does not appear in the lists of knights accompanying Vermandois.(2) Equally, it is known that many of these knights tired of the siege at Antioch and had joined Baldwin (later Baldwin I), to share in his success at Edessa.(3) André de Montbard, it would appear, was also a vassal of Champagne, so it would seem logical that both of these knights had joined Baldwin in Edessa and moved with him to Jerusalem, when he became king. Godfrey of St. Omer was presumably the son of Hugh of St. Omer. If you look at a map of France you will note that St. Omer is only a few miles from Boulogne and St. Omer was a vassal of the Boulognese House. Once again, this points to Baldwin. However, Hugh de Payen may not have been his real name (see Appendix U).

There was a Gondamar amongst the piratical crew of Guynemer who had joined Baldwin at Tarsus and, again, we know that Baldwin appropriated some three hundred of these men to help him. It would be unsurprising, therefore, had one or more of these men not been with Baldwin both at Edessa and later Jerusalem. It is possible that Bisol or Bisot, Rosal and Godfroi were part of this same group. In fact, the name was probably not Bisot, but Bigot. An Ibert Bigot (App. E, House of Giroie 2) who had married the sister of Hugh Bunel, was known to have accompanied Robert of Normandy at the siege of Jerusalem and was related to the Grantmesnils.(4) As regards Achambaud de St. Amand and Payen de Montdidier, they are both claimed to be related to the family of the Counts of Flanders, who in turn, were close family to the House of Normandy and the Counts of Boulogne. It would make sense, therefore, for them to be in the entourage either of Robert of Normandy or of Baldwin. It has been suggested on some Knights Templar sites on the Internet that Gondamar and Bisol were clergy, and had to be given permission by Bernard of Clairvaux to accept knighthood. My only comment is that I can find no original source for this statement and believe that this group was together long before 1119.

It has always seemed unlikely to me that nine unknown knights could suddenly get to the King of Jerusalem and offer their services to protect the pilgrimage routes, however, nine knights or, more likely, five knights and four men-at-arms who had served with Baldwin I, first at Edessa and later in Jerusalem, would most certainly have had access and the ear of Baldwin II. Equally, they may have been still in Edessa when Baldwin of Le Bourg, later Baldwin II, became count there. Did they seek out Baldwin II when he became king, or were they already part of his entourage? Given the period and the relative ranks, it seems to me that it was Baldwin I or II who issued the orders. But what orders? There are two possibilities and maybe a mixture of the two. The first was that Baldwin would need a bodyguard of men, preferably those who had served with him over several years and whom he trusted, not only to protect him personally, but also to take secret messages, perhaps to people of whom the majority of Franks would disapprove. For example, he certainly carried on negotiations with the Egyptian Emirs, so perhaps some of these men could speak Arabic. Certainly, many of his men learned Armenian whilst in Edessa.(5)

However, there is another interesting possibility. Undoubtedly, one of the Baldwins took over the Royal Library in Edessa, said to contain letters written by Jesus himself and his twin brother, Judas-Thomas.(6) Suppose he had found information suggesting there might be other, more important documents, hidden under the old temple grounds. The Copper Scroll (one of the Dead Sea Scrolls) appears to detail where certain documents were hidden. Did they find something similar, or even another copy? Suppose further, that he decided to look for these documents but wanted it done secretly. What better camouflage than to go to these knights and men-at-arms that he trusted and say, "I want you to look for these documents under the walls of the old temple," and remember – they still thought the mosque on the top was the original Temple of Solomon. A bit like the later Knights of the Garter, he says, "I will make you into a personal body of knights and give you the old temple as your headquarters. If anybody asks, you have asked me to set you up to protect the pilgrim routes." What perfect cover!

Let us, first of all, look at what documents the Baldwins might have found in Edessa. The Fourth Century Church historian, Eusebius, records in his *Historia Ecclesiastica*, that correspondence was exchanged between King Abgar of Edessa and Jesus, and that this correspondence was deposited in the Royal Archives where he discovered them.(7) Eusebius quoted the Abgar correspondence in full and it enjoyed great prestige in the Middle Ages. Jesus' letter was copied onto parchment and inscribed in stone. There survive a Syriac text, an Armenian version and two separate Greek versions. They do not necessarily agree in all particulars. There is a Greek version in *Acta Thaddai*. There was also a portrait of Jesus, said to be done by court painter Hannan, who is said to have visited Jesus whilst Jesus was still alive, which is mentioned in the *Doctrina Addai*.

Pope Gelasius I and a Roman Synod (c. 495 AD) rejected all of these and declared them apocryphal. Surprise, Surprise! What was the basis for their decision? They declared that *Jesus had never written anything*. So now, their Godlike being is illiterate! The idea is absurd. Jesus, whatever he may or may not have been, was a rabbi, a teacher. Of course he wrote letters. Curiously enough, the Celtic Church attached great importance to this correspondence. The *Liber Hymnorum*, which is a manuscript preserved in Trinity College, Dublin, gives two collects on the lines of the letter to Abgar.(8)

However, a glance at the letters, produced by the Church, will tell one immediately that they could not have been written in 32 AD, their supposed date. The comments by Abgar that the Jews wanted to crucify Jesus are absurd in the context. Crucifixion was a Roman punishment, not a Jewish one, which was stoning. Indeed, until the deed there was no hint that Jesus would be crucified. In fact, the whole tone of the letter is anti-Semitic, something that did not come into being until after 325 AD and the Council of Nicaea. Up to the point, where Sylvester did a deal with Constantine, Christianity had simply been considered to be a branch of Judaism and, as the Nabateaens had been converted to Judaism, it is hardly likely that a Nabataean king would be anti-Semitic. This letter therefore cannot have been written earlier than 325 AD. However, here we are faced with another problem. The legend of the letters having existed is mentioned as early as the 2nd century in the concordance of Tatian, called the *Diatessarion*, possibly as early as 110-150 AD. How do we overcome this paradox? It seems, therefore, that the letters published by the *Catholic Encyclopaedia*, and which are given in full on the Internet, are not the original ones.

It seems likely that letters were written from Edessa to Jesus, but probably by Jesus' twin brother, Judas-Thomas, on behalf of Abgar. Judas-Thomas may well have mentioned Abgar's illness and perhaps there was a letter from Jesus to his brother hoping that Abgar would recover. If Abgar then did recover, it may well have been considered miraculous and a result of Jesus' good wishes. We know from other sources that Judas-Thomas did correspond with Jesus and lived, at least for a time, in Edessa. Equally, the letters may have been written by Thaddeus, another brother of Jesus.(9) What would have really thrown a spanner in the works would have been a letter from Jesus written after 33 AD.

There is also the question of the so-called portrait, which later became a "miraculously produced" portrait that was allegedly created by Jesus putting a cloth to his face, thus imaging himself. This, of course, the Church was happy to accept. Miracles are all right – letter writing is not! This portrait became known as the "Holy Mandylion." It was stolen by Eastern Emperor Romanus Lacapenus from Edessa in 944 AD and sent to Byzantium. But was it? Did the inhabitants, in actuality, hand over a copy and keep the original? Was this found by Baldwin and did it become a proud possession of his, handed over for safe-keeping to his knights (who become the Knights Templar), with the original eventually becoming the Shroud of Turin? Now there's a thought!

What other documents could he have found? How about a copy of the original *Abdias Manuscript*? Abdias, although called "Bishop of Babylonia," was based, at least to start with, in Edessa. He was installed there probably by Judas-Thomas, Thaddeus or James, or possibly any two of them. This should surprise nobody because Edessa was founded by Nabateaens around 132 BC. The same people controlled Petra, from whence Abdias himself originated, as I have pointed out in Chapter 2. Edessa lasted until 212 AD, when it, like Petra, became a Roman province. No wonder Abdias was made Bishop there – he would be amongst his own people. It is also probable that Judas-Thomas lived there for several years, as his relics were brought back from India and interred in Edessa in 232 AD.

There also exists the possibility that there were copies of what are now known as the *Nag Hammadi Library*, or at least some of its documents. If, for example, Baldwin I had found a copy of the *Gospel of Philip*, stating Jesus was married and had a wife, this, together with the document in the hands of the Ducal House of Normandy, would have given him such a grip on the Papacy that he could almost do what he liked. Is there any proof that he had such a strong position? There is certainly some circumstantial evidence:

1. He, unlike his brother, was quite happy to accept the kingship of Jerusalem. He was not called "Guardian of the Holy Sepulchre."
2. Daimbert, the Patriarch and Papal Envoy, had been totally against Baldwin. He had wanted to establish a theocracy with himself in charge. But within two weeks after Baldwin arrived and after a private interview with Baldwin, he suddenly changed his mind, accepted Baldwin as king and agreed to consecrate him. What made him change his mind? Perhaps what Baldwin had brought with him?! Even Arnulf the ex-Patriarch was surprised.(10)
3. The most telling fact however is that in 1119, Calistus II became Pope. Calistus was the son of William, Duke of Burgundy, whose mother Adelaide had been the daughter of Richard II, Duke of Normandy.(11) This made the Papacy effectively Ulvungar or, at the very least, more amenable to Ulvungar influence, in precisely the same year that the Knights Templar were said to have been formed.

Interestingly, the two knights on horseback on the seal of the Templar's which supposedly indicated poverty may, in fact, have indicated something else – a knowledge that Jesus was one of twins – two identical knights on one horse from the same stable! And in plain sight, for everyone to see.

It is possible that Baldwin I had intended to proclaim a "New Order" with the kingdom of Jerusalem at its head, but he wanted more documentary evidence as to Jesus' family, hence the formation of the group, which became the Knights Templar and their quartering in the old temple grounds. However, we must also look at the probability that Baldwin II was the prime mover in all this. First, let us look at what documents they might have discovered. I think it likely they discovered various documents, but did not know exactly what they were.

If they did discover documents what were they likely to be? First and foremost, would have been a great many old copies of *Torah*. As the *Torah* was holy, when copies became too frayed and fragile to read, they were securely sealed in jars and buried under the temple. There would, I suspect, have been a great many, but nobody to read the Hebrew because all the Jews had been slaughtered in 1099 and I doubt than any felt safe yet to return. There may also have been the royal and priestly genealogies, which had been buried when the Turks first took Jerusalem. Again, there was nobody to read them.

However, there were Nestorian, Coptic Christian as well as Jewish colonies living in Edessa at the time that both of the Baldwins were counts there, and it would seem logical that one or the other would turn to these groups for translations of whatever was found. That person would also have been able to keep them quiet, as he had the ability to hang or behead anyone who spoke out. The Nestorians, by the way, descended from the Judaic-Christians of Edessa.

I also think that they may have started excavations before 1118, the date of the "official" founding of the Knights Templar. Whilst on this subject, there are a number of Internet sites that put the founding at 1119. This is clearly incorrect. William of Tyre states that Payens, Montbard and seven other companions had a meeting with Baldwin II in 1118 and this is confirmed by Runciman quoting both William of Tyre and other sources.(12) Baldwin I had died in 1118 without leaving a will. It was suggested that his brother, Eustace of Boulogne, should take the crown and although Eustace set out for Outremer, he was not very happy with the idea. When he was met on the way by messengers who told him that the crown had been offered and accepted by his cousin, Baldwin of Le Bourg, Count of Edessa, he turned back to France.

It is interesting that Baldwin II had previously been Count of Edessa, just as had Baldwin I. It seems that Edessa held the key. Most authorities have assumed that Baldwin II was a devout, pious member of the Catholic Church. Runciman, for example, cites the fact that he had calluses on his knees from spending so much time on them, as proof that he was pious. Today one might doubt that, as any psychologist will tell you. So let us look a little more carefully at Baldwin II's background.

Baldwin of Le Bourg, Count of Rethel, had a son Hugh, who married Melisende, daughter of Bouchard of Montlhery, Count of Corbeil and his wife Adelaide of Crecy. Bouchard of Montlhery was himself the son of Robert FitzHamon, a cousin of William the Conqueror, and he in turn had married Sybil de Montgomery, daughter of Roger de Montgomery. Roger was himself a third cousin to William I. In other words the line was pure Ulvungar. Baldwin II, the new King of Jerusalem, was the son of Hugh and Melisende.(13) Furthermore, he had married Morphia, daughter of Gabriel of Melitene, who was not Roman Catholic, but of the independent Armenian Church and he was, by all accounts, devoted to her. So all of a sudden, his so-called pious Catholicism begins to look a bit wobbly. It also accounts, perhaps, as to why he was preferred over Eustace of Boulogne for the position of king. A descendant of the two greatest Ulvungar dynasties, Normandy and Montgomery, would have been more acceptable as an Ulvungar heir than Boulogne. Robert of Normandy and Robert of Bellême had both been imprisoned by Henry I of England when Robert of Normandy had once again tried to enforce his rights to the Crown of England, and they would remain imprisoned for the rest of their lives. But an heir of both of their families now became king of the most prestigious kingdom in the Latin world. Baldwin II had been vigorously supported by Joscelin de Courtenay, Prince of Galilee, and by the Patriarch Arnulf. Joscelin was the son of another Joscelin and his wife, Isabella, who just happened to be the sister of Melisende, mother of Baldwin II. Guess what happened to Joscelin – he, too, became Count of Edessa. As one can see from the genealogies in the Appendices, the intricate marriages between the senior nobles of the Kingdom of Jerusalem are what kept the peace between neighbours, but the key seems to have been Edessa.

It is difficult for us today to understand just how important Jerusalem was to the medieval mindset. If you look at the *Mapa Mundi* in Hereford Cathedral, you will see that the centre of the map is Hierosolomita (Jerusalem), with the dome shown at its very centre.

Fig. 10-1 Modern-day Jerusalem, with the dome at its centre.

Every other known country is placed around this central point, with England right at one edge. **To the medieval mind Jerusalem was the Centre of the World and its king the most important king on Earth.**

There seems to be an assumption that for the first ten years of their existence the Knights Templar did nothing, until 1129 when Bernard of Clairvaux got involved. This is not strictly true. At least two that we know about were very close to Baldwin II, were part of his personal knights and were on campaign with him against the combined armies of the Fatimids of Egypt and Toghtekin of Damascus.(14) There were several bloody battles, many of which were not won by the Crusaders.

Baldwin himself was captured, spent two years in prison and I do not think that very much could have been done until 1124.

One thing had become obvious. The kingdom could not survive with the ordinary feudal force structure that had come with them from Europe. A band of professional soldiers was required, so Baldwin sent Hugh de Payen and André de Montbard to Europe on a recruiting campaign and to see the Pope. Unfortunately, Pope Calistus II had died by the time they reached Europe. For the time being, any idea of proclaiming a "New Order" with a Davidic/Odonic line at its head had to be abandoned. Baldwin needed the help of the new Pope.

The most important figure in ecclesiastical circles at this time was Bernard of Clairvaux. His support had enabled one Pope to overthrow another and his dispute with Abelard had resulted in the latter finishing up in a monastery. He was also the nephew of André de Montbard. Although Pope Calistus was no longer able to help, thanks to Bernard, the Order was officially sanctioned by the Church at the Council of Troyes in 1129. With this sanction, however, came a change. The Order effectively became an Order of Warrior Monks, reporting directly to the Pope. Their Grand Master was independent, no longer simply the bodyguard of the King of Jerusalem. There was undoubtedly still an inner core who knew of the documents that they had found in Edessa and Jerusalem, but the vast majority were simply warriors in the mode of the Joms-Vikings. Instead of being dedicated to Odin, they were now dedicated to "killing in the name of Christ."(15)

There is some evidence that documents were sent to Europe, as the Chancellery of the Kingdom in 1132 paid out for a box or boxes to be made of *wood, lined with oiled silk, and bound by iron, with covers of sail cloth.* Unfortunately, we don't know how big the box was, but the oiled silk suggests it was intended to keep documents damp free. Again, there is no account of what happened to this box or boxes, though it has been suggested that it was sent to Clairvaux for safekeeping.

Certainly the period from 1100 to 1133 may be considered the highest point of the success of the Ulvungar Dynasty. They ruled Scandinavia, Russia, Normandy, England, Southern Italy, North Africa and now Outremer. Unfortunately, the cost in wealth and manpower to keep all these states going was just too much, and Jerusalem, the Jewel in the Ulvungar Crown, was one venture too far.

In 1131 King Baldwin II died, leaving four daughters to succeed him – Melisende, Alice, Hodierna and Joveta. His declared heir was Melisende and it was decided that she should marry Fulk of Anjou. Alice later married Bohemond II of Antioch, Hodierna married Raymond II of Tripoli and Joveta became **Abbess of Bethany**.

Surprise! Surprise!

References
Chapter 10

1. William of Tyre (c. 1208 ed. 1934), *Die Latinische Fortsetzung* (ed. Salloch), Leipzig.
2. Runciman, *op. cit.* Chap. 3.
3. Runciman, *op.cit.* vol. I, p. 208.
4. Yeatman, J. P. (1882) - *History of the House of Arundel*, p. 20, Mitchell & Hughes, London.
5. Runciman, *op. cit.* Chap. 2.
6.. *Encyclopaedia Britannica*, 11th edition, under Abgar. Also Bauer, W. (1934, English Edition, 1971), *Orthodoxy and Heresy in Earliest Christianity.* Also Eisenman, R. (1997), *James the Brother of Jesus*, Chap. 24, Viking Penguin. Also Eusebius, circa 325 AD, *Epistle of Jesus Christ to Abgarus King of Edessa.*
7. Eusebius (c.325), *Historia Ecclesiastica*, I, xiii, Hendrickson Publishers.
8. *Liber Hymnorum MSS. E. 4, 2,* Trinity College, Dublin.
9. For both Thomas and Thaddeus see *Abdias Ms.* Book 9, Norris Collection, USA.
10. Runciman, *op. cit.* vol. I, p. 325.
11. Yeatman, J. P. (1882), *History of the House of Arundel*, p. 70, Mitchell & Hughes, London.
12. William of Tyre, *op. cit.* xii, 7, pp.520-521; and Runciman, *op. cit.* vol. II p. 157.
13. Montgomery, H., *The God-Kings of England, op. cit.* Appendix X and Runciman, *op. cit.* vol. II, App. III.
14. Fulcher of Chartres, *Gesta Francorum Iherusalem Peregrinantium*, III, ii, 1-3, pp. 314-315 (ed. Hagenmeyer 1913), Heidelberg.
15. Bernard of Clairvaux (1129), *De Laude Novae Militae.*

Chapter 11

The Angevins

In 1128, according to the chroniclers, a delegation arrived in France from Baldwin II of Jerusalem, requesting the French king to select a suitable noble to marry Baldwin's daughter Melisende and succeed Baldwin as king of Jerusalem. Louis' choice fell upon Fulk Count of Anjou, Maine and Touraine. One must ask the questions: Why was Louis asked to nominate someone? Why did he choose Fulk? Was he, in fact, only asked if he minded that a vassal of his became king of Jerusalem?

At that time, Fulk was about forty years old, was widowed and therefore free to marry and had a son Geoffrey Plantagenet. Geoffrey was both able to govern Anjou and was betrothed to Matilda, daughter and heiress of Henry I of England.

William of Tyre has this description of Fulk: "He was a ruddy man, like David, faithful and gentle, affable and kind. A powerful Prince, very successful at ruling his own people… an experienced warrior full of patience and wisdom in military affairs." His one problem, it seems, was that he had an appallingly bad memory for names and faces.(1)

The Counts of Anjou have an interesting history according to Gerald of Wales: "From the Devil they came and to the Devil they will return."(2) This refers to a legend that the Counts of Anjou were descended from the "Daughter of Satan." Odericus Vitalis said the exact same thing about Roger de Montgomery's wife, Mabel. In the case of the Counts of Anjou this was said about Melusine, the wife of the first count, whom he brought back from overseas and who presumably was not Christian. But if she was not Christian, then what was she? Was she Muslim, Jewish, a Pagan or a member of some non-Roman Catholic group such as the Elchaisites?

Let us examine all these statements a little more carefully. First and foremost, when many of the wives of the early Anjou count's names are lost, why should Melusine's be remembered? She is said to have come from overseas, but overseas in medieval times almost always meant Palestine, which was known as Outremer or Over-the-Sea.

This suggests immediately that she was either Jewish or Muslim, but it would be almost impossible for a Christian prince to meet a Muslim lady unless she was a slave, and there is no suggestion of this.

This leaves us with Jewish, but is there any other suggestion that she could have been Jewish? Yes, there is! Bishop William of Tyre said of Fulk, quoted above, "Like David." Why like David? There is no suggestion in Fulk's male ancestry that he descends from the House of David, so why would William of Tyre refer to him in this manner? Was it perhaps known that Melusine was not only Jewish, but of the House of David? Is there any other hint of this?

To examine this we need to go back to Fulk's grand-uncle, Fulk Nerra (who became Count in 987). According to the Church, Fulk Nerra was a devout man who went on pilgrimage three times to Jerusalem. Yet this count, in 992, after wining a battle, proceeded to put all of the enemy to the sword and paraded their heads on stakes. This was the count who burnt his first wife alive at the stake for infidelity.(3) This count's grand-father had likewise cut off the head of an enemy and presented it to the king of France. This sounds to me more like the doings of a worshipper of Odin, than a Christian. I accept that he might have gone on pilgrimage to atone for his sins, but *THREE TIMES*!

It should also be noted that on the first occasion he met up with Duke Robert of Normandy, who had also gone on pilgrimage (4). Both men went via Antioch and Edessa, guided by men from Antioch and Edessa, whom they met in Constantinople.(5) I do not know if Fulk visited Edessa each time he went on pilgrimage, but it is possible – after all, we all tend to return to familiar places when we go overseas.

Was Fulk looking for something? Was he looking for documents about Melusine or perhaps even descendants of her family? Was he, himself, descended from either Judas-Thomas or Thaddeus? Regretfully, I cannot provide an answer, but it seems likely! Certainly King Abgar had had a daughter called Melusine and there is no reason why she could not have had a descendant with the same name.

The reason for all the above information is that it brings into question what the chroniclers wrote and that I quoted at the beginning of this chapter. The obvious choice to marry Melisende would have been Robert of Normandy and after him, Robert de Bellême. But of these, Robert of Normandy was in prison for trying to claim the English throne from, to some, the usurper, Henry I, Robert of Normandy's youngest brother, and Robert of Bellême was dead.

Fulk's son, Geoffrey, was married to Matilda, the only surviving daughter of Henry I and heiress to both Normandy and England. One wonders, would Louis have wanted so powerful a person, whose heirs might well combine against him, to become king of Jerusalem as well? I believe that the Council of Nobles in Jerusalem wanted Fulk as the next heir, and perhaps Baldwin and others knew of Fulk's ancestry. Indeed, in Ulvungar terms this would keep the kingdoms of Jerusalem, England and the Duchy of Normandy together. So in 1154, when Henry II, Fulk's grandson, became King of England, Duke of Normandy and Count of Anjou, his half-uncle was already King of Jerusalem. This, to me, makes more sense.

At all events, Fulk went East and married Melisende and they had two sons, Baldwin and Amalric. Both of them became King of Jerusalem in turn, as Baldwin III died without heirs.(6)

A new chapter in the Ulvungar Dynasty had opened up. Henry II married Eleanor of Aquitaine, Duchess in her own right. The Angevin Empire controlled more of France than the French king. Normandy, Anjou, Maine and now Aquitaine surrounded the French Kingdom on all sides and, with the Jerusalem connection, was the most powerful force in Western Europe. They, more than anyone else, supplied knights to the land of Outremer, many of them becoming Templars.

References
Chapter 11

<u>Note:</u> *The Plantagenet Chronicles* are, in fact, a compilation of a number of chronicles and individual documents relating solely to the House of Anjou and which have been carefully put together by Dr. Elizabeth Hallam, Assistant Keeper of Medieval Records at the Public Record Office, London.

1. Hallam, E. (Editor) (1986), *The Plantagenet Chronicles*, Phoebe Philips & Macmillan Publishers, p. 38.
2. *Ibid* p. 22.
3. *Ibid* p. 25.
4. Montgomery, H., *The God-Kings of England, op. cit.* Chap. 2.
5. Hallam, *op. cit.* p. 26.
6. Runciman, *op. cit.* Vol. II, p. 492.

Chapter 12

The Odonic Line Again

In chapter 1 of the first book of this trilogy, *The God-Kings of Europe*, I introduced the Odonic Dynasty descended from the Mesopotamian God-Kings, one of whom became known as the Scandinavian god, Odin (Woden or Wotan). This dynasty included the descendants of Rhoes the Weoôulgeot and, in particular, the descendants of Ulf, King of the Visigoths or Uffe of the Mercians, who became known as Ataulf, one of the conquerors of Rome.(1) In this chapter, I am going to look further at this dynasty from another source, that of Florence of Worcester.(2)

Florence of Worcester was an 11th Century scribe, who wrote *Chronicon ex Chronicis* (or the *Chronicle of Chronicles*). As he himself acknowledges, his chronicle is based upon the chronicles of earlier writers such as the Venerable Bede and Marianus Scotus. However, whilst some of his work is clearly early Christian, some of it stems from pre-Christian works, and it is with these that we are concerned here.

According to Florence, the early British Kingdoms of Kent, East-Anglia, East-Saxons, Mercia, Deiri, West-Saxons and Lindisfari all descend from WODEN. This is clearly a pre-Christian concept – having all the kings of these lines descend from the god Woden (Odin or Wotan). According to Florence, Woden had seven sons: Wehta, Casere, Seaxnete, Weothelgeat (or Weoôulgeot) Weagdeag, Bealdeag and Winta, from whom descend these various royal kings: from Wehta, the kings of Kent; from Casere, the East-Angles; from Seaxnete, the East-Saxons; from Weothelgeat, the Mercians; from Weagdeag, the West-Saxons and Bernicians; and from Winta, the kings of Lindisfari.

Below are three of those lines, according to Florence, but it must be made clear that these are lists of kings and not necessarily genealogies.

Mercia	East-Angles	East-Saxons
WODEN	WODEN	WODEN
Weolthelgeat (or Weoôulgeot)	Casere	Seaxnete
Waga	Tytmon	Geseeg
Wihtlaeg (or Uihtlag)	Trygils	Antseeg
Wermund (Vermund or Faramund)	Hrothmund	Swaeppa
Offa (Uffe or Ulf)*	Hryp	Sigefugel
Angengeat	Wilhelm	Bedea
Eomer	Wewa (or Wehha)	Offa*
Icil	Wuffa *	Aescwine
Cnebba	Tytla	Sledda

All three lists continue and are shown in full in the relevant Appendices, but I am going to stop there for a reason. Each King List contains not only the starting point of Woden, but each contains the names Offa or Wuffa, the same name, effectively, but pronounced slightly differently by the East-Angles. We know that at various times the kingdom of Mercia was in the ascendant and its ruler acted either as Over-king or had conquered its neighbours and taken over the adjoining kingdoms. As these are King Lists and not genealogies, one would expect that the Mercian Offa or Uffe became King of Mercia before he conquered or became King of the East-Angles and East-Saxons, and before his name appeared in the other King Lists. Indeed, this is precisely what happened. He became King of Mercia before joining Alaric of the Visigoths and eventually becoming king or overlord of the whole group of Visigoths, Mercians, Angles and Saxons upon Alaric's death.

Let us now look at the Genealogy of the Visigoths or Gothic kings that I gave on page 20 of *The God-Kings of Europe,* from sources other than Florence of Worchester and compare them to the Mercian list:

Visigothic Kings Genealogy	Mercian Kings (per Florence)
Rhoes the Weoôulgeat*	Weolthelgeot*
Chattaric the Uihtlag**	Waga
Vermund or Faramund***	Wihtlaeg (or Uihtlag)**
Uffe or Ulf****	Wermund or Vermund***
Hlodio	Offa****
Hlodovech	Angengeat

The two lists speak for themselves. It is perfectly apparent that we are looking at two lists, but effectively the same family of Mercian kings, who were also leaders of the whole of the Visigothic realms and which included most of France, the Spanish March and large chunks of England.

Alaric, the King of the Visigoths, had married Uffe's sister, the daughter of Vermund, and one assumes that Uffe accompanied his sister to her wedding with Alaric and then decided to accompany Alaric when he sacked Rome, an opportunity to plunder too good to miss. When Alaric died then Ulf, as he was called in Visigothic, became king of the Visigoths as well.

However I do not think it likely that Uffe (Ulf) would have left his British domains without securing a successor of his own blood. Almost certainly, he would have married prior to his sister and had a child or children before embarking on the journey to the South.

Map 1.
Approximate positions of the kingdoms at the time of Ataulf

Most scholars agree that Angengeat was probably the son of Uffe and Aescwine may be his son or even the same person with a slightly different name in East-Saxon. This means, of course, that there are two totally separate Ulvungar dynasties (on the basis that Ulvungars descend from Ulf) – a Visigothic one descended from Ulf and Maria, and a Mercian one descended from Uffe and an unknown wife. Tellingly, the line of the West-Saxons (Wessex) and the lines of Kent and Northumbria do not contain the Uffe lineage. However, the importance of Ulf's marriage to Maria cannot be overemphasised. She descended from every Royal Judaic Dynasty, the Davidic Line from Jesus, the Saulic and Herodian lines from Saul/Sigismundus and the Hasmodean and Petran lines from John the Baptist.

We must now consider the vexed question of Woden's ancestors, because Florence gives a genealogy which takes Woden back to a person called Seth:

SETH

Beadwi

Wala

Hathra

Itermod

Heremod

Sceadwala

Beaw

Cetwa

Geta

Godwlf

Finn

Frithowlf

Frealaf

Frithewald

WODEN

I am sure that Florence, when he copied this down from pre-Christian documents, assumed that Seth was the Biblical Seth, the third son of Adam after the murder of Abel and the father of Enos. But actually, is this likely?

The pre-Christian writers would have had no knowledge of an obscure Semitic Book called *Torah*. They would have known nothing about Adam and Eve, the Garden of Eden or Seth or his son Enos. And anyway, if this was intended, then why not state "Seth, the son of Adam, father of Enos" and give the biblical genealogy? Clearly, too, there are simply not enough generations between Woden and Seth. The grandson of Woden, Chattaric the Uihtlag, died in 381 AD, which places Woden about 250-320 AD. If we take the usual thirty years per generation, it would take us no further back than 200 BC.

Here, however, we must be careful. Our ancestors did not necessarily look at thirty years as equalling a generation. St. Mathew's gospel, it is generally agreed, uses about seventy-five years per generation and there are clearly names missed out. The Elchasaic Document on page 35 of the *God-Kings of Europe* has the same problem. Furthermore, early Biblical writers tended to use one hundred years as a generation, based upon the statement in Genesis 6:3, *"Yet his days shall be an hundred and twenty years."* In fact, the Anglo-Saxons also used one hundred years per generation or *"hund cnect,"* which can be translated as "one hundred generations" or "a hundred generation." In particular, this was applied to their belief that the city of London had been built by giants – *"enta geweorc"* – a hundred years ago.(3)

If, therefore, we apply one hundred years to each of these generations, then we can go back to about 1,200 BC. But does this help us? Was there someone called Seth around in 1,200 BC from whom this family might descend? Well, yes there was! His name was Seth, or Seti I, and he was King of Egypt, or pharaoh.

At first sight, it seems highly unlikely that this could be the Seth referred to, but the more I investigated the more likely it became. Seti means "He of the god Seth." In other words, he was dedicated to the god Seth or Set. It is worthwhile to look at who this God was and why a pharaoh should have been dedicated to him.

According to the work of Caroline Seawright and Lorraine Turner, Set (variants: Seth, Setekh, Sut and Suty) (4), was one of Egypt's most ancient and earliest gods. He was a god of confusion, chaos, storms, wind, the desert and of *foreign lands*. In the Osiris legends he was a contender for the throne of Osiris, a rival to the god Horus, but companion to the god Ra. Certain fish were sacred to Seth – for example the Nile carp, the oxyrynchus or phagrus fish. This was because they believed that these fish had eaten the male genital organs of Osiris after Seth chopped him into little pieces. Seth was also believed to be white with red hair and animals that were red were thought to be his followers, as were people with red hair.

Seth was believed by the Egyptians to be infertile. In his battle with Horus, the latter was supposed to have torn off Seth's testicles whilst, in turn, Seth was supposed to have torn out Horus's eye. He was also supposed to be bisexual or possibly homosexual. He is said to have tried to seduce Horus with the words, "How lovely your backside is!" Originally, he was seen as almost a twin to Horus the Elder. Horus ruled the day sky, whilst Seth ruled the night sky. In the Pyramid texts (Pepi I) it states: "Homage to thee O Ladder of Seth! Stand thou upright O Ladder of Horus!"
On one of Seti I's reliefs, it shows Seth and Horus offering the symbol of life to the pharaoh, with Seth saying: "I establish the crown upon your head, even like the disk of Amen-Ra and I will give you life strength and health."

Ramesses II and Seti I both had red hair and so chose Set as their particular god. Ramesses is compared to Seth in the account of the battle of Qedesh, which is to be found in the Ramesseum: "His majesty was like Seth, great-of-strength." It was not until a later period when Horus, son of Isis, and Horus the Elder became confused so that Set came to be considered evil. Originally, Seth had been the Lord of Lower Egypt just as Horus the Elder had been the Lord of Upper Egypt. Set was also seen as the protector of Ra. It was he who defended the solar barque as it made its way through the underworld. Seth was the only God who could kill Apep, the serpent, and Ra's most dangerous enemy. Compare this with the Saga of Ragnar Lothbroc, the great serpent killer. Ragnar Lothbroc is supposedly descended from Seth via Woden.

Seth was also believed to live in the constellation of the Great Bear, in the North, symbolising darkness and cold. The Hyksos, who may well have been the Hebrews, took Seth as their main god after the expulsion of foreigners from Egypt. If the Hebrews were the same as the Hyksos, then it is likely that Moses' full name was Set-Moses. Interestingly, Seth was given, as wives or concubines, Anat and Astarte or Asherah, the daughters of Ra, who were both war goddesses from the Syria-Palestine area. Asherah was, of course, later to become associated with the Hebrew Yahweh.

But how does this help us? Ramesses I and Seti I, his son by Queen Sitre, were the founders of the 19th Dynasty (1342-1197 BC), though the chronology may differ between Egyptian scholars. Seti I was pharaoh from either 1294-1279 BC or 1290-1279 BC, dependent upon which chronology is used. He and his father had the problem of clearing up the Egyptian religion after the heretical *One Only God* Aten, and the pharaohs who supported him, were overthrown. They then had to restore the worship of Amen-Ra, Osiris, Min, Seth and the remainder of the Egyptian pantheon. This was also the time when Egypt was successful against the Hittites under their great war-pharaohs, Ramesses I, Seti I, and Ramesses II. Indeed, Egypt reached the apex of its greatness under these pharaohs. It was also the time of the Kassite Dynasty of Babylon under their kings Adad-Shuma-Iddina (1225-1219 BC), the first of the Kassite Kings to be called Iddina or Odin. In 1174 Marduk-Apla-Iddina came to the throne, followed in 1161 by Zababa-Shuma-Iddina, who ruled until 1160 BC and was the last, but one, of the Kassite dynasty. The Egyptians, meanwhile, had not only regained Syria and Palestine from the Hittites, but also made themselves masters of the Middle East. This was acknowledged by the Babylonian rulers, who gave their daughters to the pharaohs as wives and, in turn, accepted daughters of the pharaoh as wives.

In *The God-Kings of Europe*, I showed that when the Kassite Dynasty was overthrown, its members trekked northwards, their descendants eventually becoming the Goths of Scandinavia, and that this could be shown by the Icelandic epic *Hyndlujóo* (5) and could be confirmed genetically by the genetic mutation CCR5-delta 32. Since then, a large DNA study, which is still ongoing, seems to confirm this.

If, therefore, a daughter of Seti I had married one of the kings of the Kassite Dynasty and their descendants had eventually settled in Scandinavia, it would not be surprising if they remembered vaguely a warrior king called Seth and put him at the beginning of their ancestral line – just as a later famous warrior king, Woden, was put at the beginning of the lines of the English kings. Just as Woden became mythologized into a Scandinavian god, so probably the god Seth and Seti I became confused, and Seth's action of putting out the eye of Horus became associated with Odin (Woden) losing an eye.

However, one must not dismiss the Biblical Seth. Rashi (Rabbi Shlomo Yitzhaqi) refers to Seth as the father of Noah and the ancestor of all of the generations of the Tzaddikim, the righteous ones. There was also a Gnostic school called the "Sethians," which appears to have focused on Seth as the righteous one and a precursor to Jesus.
In fact, it occurred to me that the Egyptian Seth and the Biblical Seth may be one and the same.

Furthermore, in the first-century *Gospel of Judas*, which has recently been translated into English by Pagels and King, Judas states that Jesus comes from the realm of the immortal Barbelo, the Divine mother of Egyptian Sethian-Christianity, which maintains that the spiritual human race descends from Seth, the third son of Adam and that the trinity is the Divine Father (Invisible Spirit), the Divine Mother (Barbelo) and the Divine Son (Autogenes or Christ).(6) This, of course, echoes the older Egyptian Osiris-Isis-Horus trinity.

As explained in *The God-Kings of Europe*, it is highly unlikely that the story of the flood and much of Genesis can predate the Babylonian exile and that the earliest form of Judaism was the Haggadic tradition, or the exodus from Egypt. If you had been a worshipper of the one God, Aten (Adam?) in the form of his god-on-earth, the pharaoh Akhnaten, and his wife Nefertiti (Eve) and if you had been chucked out of the wonderful paradise of Akhnaten, and been forced to leave Egypt, would you not perhaps have reverted to worshipping the god of foreign lands, Seth, and would not perhaps your leader have taken the name Seth-Moses, the replacement for the lost son, Tutenkhaten (Abel), who was forced to become Tutenkhamun by his brother, the high priest of Amun (Cain)? This is merely an idea, but it seems logical.

Graham Phillips in his books, *Act of God* and *Legacy of Moses*, makes a persuasive case for the Exodus taking place as a result of the eruption of the Thera volcano at about 1359-1370 BC and that there were two Moses – one being Ka-Moses, who was a priest and gave the Israelites their One-God religion, and the second, Thuth-Moses, who was a renegade prince of Egypt and who led them out of captivity. This, however, does not invalidate my idea of one of them taking the name Seth-Moses.(7)

If one now goes to Document 4 which I gave on page 124 of *The God-Kings of Europe* (Appendix C), then it becomes clear that you have an Isis, Osiris, Horus, Seth legend upon which has been overlaid an early, part-Christian part-pagan story, but which became part of the folklore of the Ulvungar Dynasty. Thus, Mary of Bethany is shown as a priestess of Isis. She is of the Tribe of Benjamin, who were mercenary warriors of the pharaoh and living on Elephantine Island, the island of Isis. This, in turn, became the Temple of the Zadoks, of which Jesus' family were members. The line of Odin claimed descent from Seth, an Egyptian god-king, and when these two lines conjoined, a fusion of each of these two family legends and the two Seths gradually became a type of joint mythology. How much of this is true or not is irrelevant; what it produced was a belief that this dynasty was destined to become kings, not only of Europe, but of their ancient Kingdom of Syria and Palestine – OUTREMER.

In the years 318-325 AD the Roman Empire and the Papacy had made Roman Christianity the only religion of the Roman Empire and had thereby disinherited the idea of god-kingship, whether Odonic, Egyptian or Mesopotamian, and had written the family of Jesus out of history. In 412 AD, Rome had been sacked by Alaric and Ataulf, and Ataulf had married Maria of the family of Jesus. By 700 AD the grip of Rome on religion was weakening. The Papacy countered by making Charlemagne "Holy Roman Emperor" in 800 AD and with a vigorous baptising campaign. Seven hundred years later, in 1119, the Ulvungar descendants were kings or rulers of all of Scandinavia, Russia, Normandy, England, Scotland, Anjou, Maine, Touraine, Toulouse, Aquitaine, Southern Italy, Sicily, North Africa, Edessa, Antioch, Jerusalem and had installed their own man as Pope. The grip of the Roman Papacy once again was on the decline. A century later, with the support of the Ulvungars, the Cathars were shaking Roman theology to its foundations. Once again, the Roman Church counter-attacked with the Albigensian Crusade and tried to stamp out the idea that Jesus was married and had children. The Templars gave refuge to many Cathars, then they themselves were attacked, this time by a greedy King of France and his tame Pope.

References:
Chapter 12

1. Montgomery, *op. cit.*(2006) Chap. 1
2. I have used photocopies of a rare manuscript copy of Florence of Worchester's work, published in 1854 by Henry Bohn, edited and partially translated by Thomas Forrester. It was in the library of my late cousin, Count Bo-Gabriel de Montgomery of Djursholm, Sweden, and is now in the possession of his daughter, Sophie, who kindly enlarged and photocopied the relevant pages for me.
3. Ackroyd, P. (2001), *London, The Biography*, p. 31, Vintage Books.
4. Seawright, C. (2007), *Set (Seth), God of Storms, Slayer of Apep, Equal to and Rival of Horus*, Turner, L. (2006), *Lectures in Egyptology*, Uttoxeter and District U3A.

>>Seth (Hebrew: שֵׁת, Standard Šet, Tiberian Šē□; Arabic: شِيث Shith or Shiyth; "Placed; appointed in the Book of Genesis of the Hebrew Bible, is the third listed son of Adam and Eve and brother Cain and Abel

http://www.touregypt.net/featurestories/set.htm.
5. Montgomery, *op. cit.* Chapter 1.
6. Pagels, E. & King, K. L. (2007), *Reading Judas*, pp. 110 & 133, Allen Lane (Penguin).
7. Phillips, G. (1998), *Act of God*, and *The Moses Legacy* (2002), Pan Books.

Chapter 13

The End of the Kingdom of Jerusalem and the Knights Templar

In August of 1291 the last bastion of the Kingdom of Outremer fell, with the fall of Acre. The dream of the Ulvungar Dynasty to rule their world from its centre, Jerusalem, was over, but some at least had foreseen this eventuality and prepared against it.

The Knights Templar had been created to protect the Dynasty and its secrets, and no, I do not believe in the Priory of Zion! The Knights Templar were an Ulvungar creation, dedicated to "the obedience of Bethany,"(1) first under the Baldwins and then Fulk. Early on, it had been recognised that to continue the struggle, a professional group of Knights was needed, based upon the ideas of the Joms-Vikings and the Varangian Guard. But to be successful they not only had to be trained, they needed wealth to keep them and their entourages.

Bernard of Clairvaux, the foremost churchman of his time and the nephew of André de Montbard, had been enlisted to help make the Templars acceptable to the Church and to gain them recruits. Yes – there were now members who were no longer "family," but there were always family members in senior positions. What happened to the documents that I believe they found? I think most ended up in the Abbey of Cluny, where they were carefully copied out by clerks who were sworn to secrecy. It seems likely that some of these documents ended up with members of the Ulvungars and their descendants.

I think also that many Ulvungars blamed their defeat on the Catholic Church and decided that they would do all in their power to bring it down. That they supported the Cathars is without doubt. The Cathars were the direct descendants of the Elchasaites, from whom the Ulvungars themselves sprang – indeed, the word Cathar comes from the word *katharioi*,(2) used to describe the Elchasaites. The Cathars, like the Elchasaites, claimed to have written proof that Jesus was married, and who indeed had two wives, one of whom was Mary Magdalene.(3) It was one of the major reasons for the Crusade against the Cathars in 1209, which lasted until 1229, and is known as the

Albigensian Crusade. This crusade attempted to wipe out not only the believers in this alternate version of Christianity but, in particular, to destroy all their documents. It nearly succeeded!

The Templars refused to take part, because the Ulvungar Counts of Toulouse were the protectors of the Cathars and, being senior members of the Templars themselves, almost certainly knew the truth. Eventually, the Templars themselves came under attack. Once again, the Church was trying to kill off the members of The Family and destroy their documents, although now it was also greed that helped to fuel this particular purge.

The Ulvungar families were certainly behind the Renaissance and the interest in ancient manuscripts from Greek and Roman times. What one must remember is that many of the families of Outremer had lived there for several generations and had never seen Europe. To them Outremer was "home;" many of them spoke Arabic and had learned from Islamic scholars. They may have fought the Saracens, but they also learned from them. Arab doctors were much sought after for their medical skill. The same must be said of the Kingdom of Sicily. Some, at least, had learned from the great Islamic scholars such as Uthman al-Jahith (781-869), whose *Book of Animals* and theory of natural selection predated Darwin's theory of the *Origin of the Species* by one thousand years and was heresy, of course, to the Church. Uthman was an Arab of East African descent. For over seven hundred years the language of science was Arabic. Take, for example, the House of Wisdom of Al-Ma'mun, the greatest university in the world since Alexandria. Even when the scientists and philosophers were not themselves Arabs, they conducted their researches and studies and wrote in Arabic, such as the great mathematician al-Khwarizmi or the philosopher al-Kindi. The greatest medical textbook of the Middle Ages was called the *Canon of Medicines* and was written by ibn Sina, who was born in Persia in 980 AD. Another Persian scholar, al-Biruni, developed the mathematics of trigonometry and was able to measure the circumference of the Earth to within a few miles. With the sacking of Baghdad in 1258 by the Mongols, the days of Baghdad as a centre of scientific thought were over, but it nevertheless continued in places like Cordoba and Sicily.

The Templars, in particular, learned trigonometry and geometry and the masons who worked for them soon learned this as well. Indeed, the idea of squaring the circle comes from these studies. Were they also behind the establishment of Freemasonry? I think it very likely, but do not think that one should necessarily look for the continuation of the Templars in Freemasonry alone.

It would have been continued within the families who made up the Ulvungar Dynasty. It would continue in the Valois, St. Clair, Beaumont and Montgomery families, to name but a few. It resulted in the establishment of the Kingdom of the Teutonic Knights, an offshoot of the Templars and the Kingdom of Prussia, whose rulers became German emperors. The Teutonic Knights, whose full name was *Hospitalis Sancte Marie Alemannorum Jerosolimitani,* were an offshoot of the Knights Templars made up of mostly German Knights, based originally at Acre and founded in 1190 as a hospice brotherhood. It became very powerful after the establishment of the Ordenstaat during the 13th Century, which lasted until 1525. After the fall of Acre the headquarters of the order was moved to Venice, but in 1309 the headquarters was moved again to Marienburg. The Grand Master of the Order had complete control over Prussia and was not only the castellan of Marienburg Castle, but also a member of the Hanseatic League.

However, in 1525, the then Grand Master, Albert of Brandenburg-Ansbach, converted to Lutheranism and turned the Ordenstaat into the secular Lutheran Duchy of Prussia. This, in turn, became later the Kingdom of Prussia and with the unification of Germany on the 1st of January, 1871, the King of Prussia became the Emperor of Germany. This would eventually cause the First World War, with the most terrible consequences for the Ulvungar dynasty.

The Ulvungars were undoubtedly involved in the creation of Protestantism, the non-conformist movements and, in particular, the Unitarian movement.

I mentioned also in *The God-Kings of Europe* the question of the goddess line and the sacred triangle. It is worthwhile noting that the wife of William I, Matilda of Flanders, was either married before she married William, or was living with a lover. The work of J. P. Yeatman, who did considerable researches both at Belvoir Castle and in France, points inexorably to the fact that Matilda had several children prior to her marriage with William. Unfortunately, most of these documents were destroyed during the first and second world wars, so one is particularly lucky that some of his researches were printed in 1882. Matilda's first husband or lover appears to have been called either Gherbod or Brictric, though the latter may be the name adopted by the English branch of this family. The only son known was certainly called Gherbod, and was made Earl of Chester by William after the conquest prior to Hugh the Fat (in Domesday he is called nephew), and there were two known daughters, Gundred, who married William de Warren, and Matilde, who married Roger de Busli. It seems, therefore, that William had no difficulty in recognising his wife's previous relationship, though the Church disapproved and said that they were "living in adultery." The sacred triangle appears to have operated at the very heart of the Ulvungar Dynasty.(4)

The Templars, too, had their continuators. Just as they were the continuators of the Benjamite Mercenaries, the Joms-Vikings and the Varangian Guard, so, too, the great mercenary companies of the hundred years war and other wars in Europe are the continuators of the Templars – companies such as The Great Company, The White Company, Companie de Gentilhommes d'Armes Ecossais, the Scots Guards of France and the various Italian Condottiori, some of which continued up until 1782.

This book, however, must end here. I have shown in this trilogy how the Ulvungars originated and how they, through force of arms, conquered most of the then known world, finally achieving their goal of reigning in Jerusalem, only to lose Outremer two hundred years later. Nonetheless, for two hundred years the Ulvungar Dynasty ruled over most of France, Spain, Southern Italy, England, Scotland, Russia and all of Scandinavia and well as large chunks of Africa and the Middle East. Not until the British Empire would one family control so much again and, of course, the British Royal Family are descendants of the Ulvungars.

References
Chapter 13

1. Bernard of Clairvaux commended the Knights Templar to "The Obedience of Bethany, the castle of Mary and Martha."
2. Stoyanov, Y. *op. cit.* p. 87.
3. *Ibid* p. 223.
4. Yeatman, J. P. (1882), *History of the House of Arundel*, p. 38, Mitchell & Hughes.

APPENDIX A

THE COHEN MODAL HAPLOTYPE

A couple of notes on the Cohen Modal Haplotype:

THE COHEN MARKERS /
DYS19/DYS394 = 14 / 14
DYS**385a** = 13 / 13
DYS**385b** = 15 / *18*
DYS388 = 16 / *15*
DYS389-1 = 13 / 13
DYS389-2 = 30 / *29*
DYS390 = 23 / 23
DYS391 = 10 / 10
DYS392 = 11 / 11
DYS393 = 12 / 12
DYS426 = 11 / 11
DYS**439** = 21 / *11*

Those results shown in italics are mutations (genetic distance).
Those DYS numbers shown in bold are known to mutate much faster
than the norm and so any mutation on these markers is not taken as
seriously as on the black markers.

The 12 marker Cohen Modal Haplotype (CMH-12) is based upon
studies by a private company. It has not been peer group reviewed by
other scientists or published in the open technical literature. It is the
6 marker Cohen Modal Haplotype (CMH-6) that is the basis for cur-
rent technical publications. These markers (CMH-6) are given by:

DYS19 = 14 / 14
DYS388 = 16 / *15*
DYS390 = 23 / 23
DYS391 = 10 / 10
DYS392 = 11 / 11
DYS393 = 12 / 12

The Cohen Modal Haplogroup (CMH) is a subgroup of haplogroup J. Although you can have the CMH in either J1 or J2, it is the genetic signature in J1 that is considered the Jewish priestly signature. However, being a genetic distance of one from this, even on a black marker, is not considered too significant.

While Kohanim are believed to have descended in the patrilineal line from Aaron, brother of Moses, Levites (a second level of Jewish priesthood) are traditionally believed to have descended in the patrilineal line from Levi, son of Jacob. Levites should also, therefore, share common Y-chromosomal DNA.

There is also work published in the American Journal of Human Genetics about the Cohen Modal Haplotype and the origins of the Lemba, the Black Jews of South Africa, which suggests that there were black-African Jews from the very beginning and that some went south into what is now South Africa at the time of the Exodus. See Thomas, M.; Parfitt, T.; Weiss, D. A.; Skorecki, K.; Wilson, J. F.; le Roux, M.; Bradman, N.; Goldstein, D. B. (2000), *T Chromosomes Travelling South: the Cohen Modal Haplotype and the Origins of the Lemba - The Black Jews of Southern Africa*, American Journal of Human Genetics, Feb. 2000, No. 66.

APPENDIX B

The Codes of Protection and the Dating of
The House of Bethany Document

After 325 AD the family of Jesus was under attack from both the Roman Church and the Roman state. Malachi Martin says that many changed their names or fled, but it was a little more clever than that. There was one main line to be protected: the line of Saul/Paul and Mary, daughter of Jesus and Mary of Bethany, whose daughter, Ruth, had married her half-uncle, John Matinus, who was of course the youngest son of Jesus and Mary Magdalene.

This meant giving codes to Paul, John and Ruth. These were as follows:

a. Saul/Paul became "Sigismundus." *Sig* in Latin is short for Signo or Signum. The first means "seal" or "sign," or even "to make the sign of the cross +."

Is is Latin for "He." *Mundus* is Latin for "World." Therefore, Sig-Is-Mundus = **He is the Sign for the World** or even the **cross of the world**.

b. John Matinus or Martinus became "Osmeus." *Os* is Latin for Face or Speech, whilst *Meus* means My. Therefore, his code name meant My Face or My Speech. So he was either the Face of Jesus perhaps because he looked like him or he was Jesus' spokesman.

c. Ruth became "Muriel." *Muri* is the colour purple from the Latin word Murex, indicating that she was of the Royal Blood, whilst *El* is one of the Hebrew names for God. As it was the Church itself that had proclaimed Jesus to be God, it would perfectly suit the Jewish humour to proclaim that she was Born to the Purple and descended from the God-Jesus, the Royal Mother – however, this Code was not used for Ruth until much later.

Os can also mean "Word." According to Barbara Thiering, the pesher code used when Jesus had any children was "The *word* of the

Lord increased." Jesus is also often referred to as The Word, so once again they are using meanings within meanings.

There were other code words as well, but these are important to understanding the genealogies.

We can say, therefore, that the document called *The House of Bethany* was produced after 325 AD. It was, however, produced before Ruth became Muriel and it shows Meroveus as the heir of Clodimir. However, Meroveus the Younger died in 430 AD at the battle of Soissons, without heirs, and his brother Hlodovech became the heir.

Introduction to Appendices C & D

Appendix C – *The Legend of Mary Magdalene* is actually about Mary of Bethany, but during the early 13th Century it was assumed that Mary of Bethany, Mary Magdalene and Mary the Penitent were all one and the same person because Pope Gregory had declared it to be in one of his homilies. It was not until the 1960s that the Catholic Church acknowledged that the Pope had been wrong all along. This, however, caused considerable problems and both Appendices show the same mistake.

It is known that the document shown in Appendix C was around in the south of France in various forms at the time of the Albigensian Crusade (1209). It seems likely that the Archbishop of Genoa, Jacobus de Voraigne, wrote *The Golden Legend* (*Aurea Legenda* – Appendix D) in 1275 to combat the earlier one and try to refute it.

The original Appendix D is in the Fordham University Center for Medieval Studies. This is the Caxton English translation of 1470 (Edition 1483) as edited by Ellis in 1900 and subsequently reprinted in 1931.

To those unfamiliar with the medieval mindset and way of expressing themselves, the English in Appendix D may seem unwieldy and strange. Various words have a somewhat different meaning to those commonly associated with them today. Mary is said to be bitter because she is repenting her ways as a prostitute, although there was never the slightest evidence for this outside of Pope Gregory's homily.

I have deliberately not attempted to change the English and update it. Appendix C is a 17th Century English translation, so is easier to understand than Appendix D. Most of the words will be familiar to the reader.

Appendix C

The Legend of Mary Magdalene

"Now it came to pass in those days that a Priestess of the Goddess from the village of Bethany of the Tribe of Benjamin and a keeper of the Sacred Doves was affianced to a man called Jeshua for she had served her six years. Now Jeshua was of the House of David the King and they were married.

And Jeshua rebelled against the oppressors against Rome and was defeated, but many Romans were devotees of the Mother and were unwilling to kill her priestess who was with child. So Miriam took ship and was secretly smuggled into Gaul where she was delivered and there she abode many years. Now she bore a daughter who was exceedingly fair and the King of that place looked upon her and demanded that she be his wife but she was promised to the Goddess. But the King would not have it so and took her and made her his wife and she bore him a son and a daughter.

But the Goddess was exceeding wrath for his rape of her daughter and cursed him saying, 'Thy seed shall be estranged from me and thine inheritance taken from thee. Thy seed shall end by the piercing of an eye and so shall thine inheritance cease.

Yet for the sake of my priestess whom thou ravished shall I forgive thee and thy seed if they fulfil those labours which I shall give them.

They must fight and capture that which was lost to the oppressors of thy wife though they shall not hold it for they shall suffer betrayal (as thou betrayed me). Unless one of thy seed shall end the House of their betrayers by piercing the eye of its Liege. To this family shall I award greatness if they return to me and from this time to that shall be four and one hundred generations..'"

<u>Appendix D</u>

Here followeth the life of S. Mary Magdalene, and first of her name.

Mary is as much to say as bitter, or a lighter, or lighted. By this be understood three things that be three, the best parts that she chose. That is to say, part of penance, part of contemplation within forth, and part of heavenly glory. And of this treble part is understood that is said by our Lord: Mary hath chosen the best part, which shall not be taken from her. The first part shall not be taken from her because of the end, which is the following of blessedness; the second because of continuance, for the continuance of her life is continued with the contemplation of her country. The third by reason of perdurableness; and forasmuch as she chose the best part of penance, she is said: a bitter sea, for therein she had much bitterness. And that appeared in that she wept so many tears that she washed therewith the feet of our Lord. And for so much as she chose the part of contemplation withinforth, she is a lighter, for there she took so largely that she spread it abundantly. She took the light there, with which after she enlumined other, and in that she chose the best part of the heavenly glory, she is called the light. For then she was enlumined of perfect knowledge in thought, and with the light in clearness of body. Magdalene is as much as to say as abiding culpable. Or Magdalene is interpreted as closed or shut, or not to be overcome. Or full of magnificence, by which is showed what she was tofore her conversion, and what in her conversion, and what after her conversion. For tofore her conversion she was abiding guilty by obligation to everlasting pain. In the conversion she was garnished by armour of penance. She was in the best wise garnished with penance. For as many delices as she had in her, so many sacrifices

were found in her. And after her conversion she was prai-
sed by overabundance of grace. For whereas sin abounded,
grace overabounded, and was more, etc.

Of Mary Magdalene

Mary Magdalene had her surname of Magdalo, a castle,
and was born of right noble lineage and parents, which
were descended of the lineage of kings. And her father was
named Cyrus, and her mother Eucharis. She with her brother Lazarus, and her sister Martha, possessed the castle of
Magdalo, which is two miles from Nazareth, and Bethany,
the castle which is nigh to Jerusalem, and also a great part
of Jerusalem, which, all these things they departed among
them. In such wise that Mary had the castle Magdalo, whe-
reof she had her name Magdalene. And Lazarus had the
part of the city of Jerusalem, and Martha had to her part
Bethany. And when Mary gave herself to all delights of the
body, and Lazarus entended all to knighthood, Martha,
which was wise, governed nobly her brother's part and
also her sister's, and also her own, and administered to
knights, and her servants, and to poor men, such necessities as they needed. Nevertheless, after the ascension of our
Lord, they sold all these things, and brought the value thereof, and laid it at the feet of the apostles. Then when
Magdalene abounded in riches, and because delight is fellow to riches and abundance of things; and for so much as
she shone in beauty greatly, and in riches, so much the
more she submitted her body to delight, and therefore she
lost her right name, and was called customably a sinner.
And when our Lord Jesu Christ preached there and in other
places, she was inspired with the Holy Ghost, and went
into the house of Simon leprous, whereas our Lord dined.
Then she durst not, because she was a sinner, appear tofore the just and good people, but remained behind at the feet
of our Lord, and washed his feet with the tears of her eyes

and dryed them with the hair of her head, and anointed them with precious ointments. For the inhabitants of that region used baths and ointments for the overgreat burning and heat of the sun. And because that Simon the Pharisee thought in himself that, if our Lord had been a very prophet, he would not have suffered a sinful woman to have touched him, then our Lord reproved him of his presumption, and forgave the woman all her sins. And this is she, that same Mary Magdalene to whom our Lord gave so many great gifts. And showed so great signs of love, that he took from her seven devils. He embraced her all in his love, and made her right familiar with him. He would that she should be his hostess, and his procuress on his journey, and he ofttimes excused her sweetly; for he excused her against the Pharisee which said that she was not clean, and unto her sister that said she was idle, unto Judas, who said that she was a wastresse of goods. And when he saw her weep he could not withhold his tears. And for the love of her he raised Lazarus which had been four days dead, and healed her sister from the flux of blood which had held her seven years. And by the merits of her he made Martelle, chamberer of her sister Martha, to say that sweet word: Blessed be the womb that bare thee, and the paps that gave thee suck. But, after S. Ambrose, it was Martha that said so, and this was her chamberer. This Mary Magdalene is she that washed the feet of our Lord and dried them with the hair of her head, and anointed them with precious ointment, and did solemn penance in the time of grace, and was the first that chose the best part, which was at the feet of our Lord, and heard his preaching. Which anointed his head; at his passion was nigh unto the cross; which made ready ointments, and would anoint his body, and would not depart from the monument when his disciples departed. To whom Jesu Christ appeared first after his resurrection, and was fellow to the apostles, and made of our Lord apostolesse of the apostles, then after the ascension of our Lord, the fourteenth year from his passion, long after that the Jews had slain S. Stephen, and had cast out the other disciples out of the Jewry, which went into divers countries, and preached the word of God. There was that time with the apostles S. Maximin, which was one of the seventy-two disciples of our Lord, to whom the blessed Mary Magdalene was committed by S. Peter, and then, when the disciples were departed, S. Maximin, Mary Magdalene, and Lazarus her brother, Martha her sister, Marcelle, chamberer of Martha, and S. Cedony which was born blind, and after enlumined of our Lord; all these together, and many other christian men were taken of the miscreants and put in a ship in the sea, without any tackle or rudder, for to be drowned. But by the purveyance of Almighty God they came all to Marseilles, where, as none would receive them to be lodged, they dwelled and abode under a porch tofore a temple of the people of that country. And when the blessed Mary Magdalene saw the people assembled at this temple for to do sacrifice to the idols, she arose up peaceably with a glad visage, a discreet tongue and well speaking, and began to preach the faith and law of Jesu Christ, and withdrew from the worshipping of the idols. Then were they amarvelled of the beauty, of the reason, and of the fair speaking of her. And it was no marvel that the mouth that had kissed the feet of our Lord so debonairly and so goodly, should be inspired with the word of God more than the other. And after that, it happed that the prince of the province and his wife made sacrifice to the idols for to have a child. And Mary Magdalene preached to them Jesu Christ and forbade them those sacrifices. And after that a little while, Mary Magdalene appeared in a vision to that lady, saying: Wherefore hast thou so much riches and sufferest the poor people our Lord to die for hunger and for cold? And she doubted, and was afraid to show this vision to her lord. And then the second night she appeared to her again and said in likewise and adjousted thereto menaces, if she warned not her husband for to comfort the poor and needy, and yet she said nothing thereof to her husband. And then she appeared to her the third night, when it was dark, and to her husband also, with a frowning and angry visage like fire, like as all the house had burned, and said: Thou tyrant and member of thy father the devil, with that serpent thy wife, that will not say to thee my words, thou restest now enemy of the cross, which hast filled thy belly by gluttony, with divers manner of meats and sufferest to perish for hunger the holy saints of our Lord. Liest thou not in a palace wrapped with clothes of silk. And thou seest them without harbour, discomforted, and goest forth and takest no regard to them. Thou shalt not escape so ne depart without punishment, thou tyrant and felon because thou hast so long tarried. And when Mary Magdalene had said thus she departed away. Then the lady awoke and sighed. And the husband sighed strongly also for the same cause, and trembled.

And then she said: Sir, hast thou seen the sweven that I have seen? I have seen, said he, that I am greatly amarvelled of, and am sore afraid what we shall do. And his wife said: It is more profitable for us to obey her, than to run into the ire of her God, whom she preacheth. For which cause they received them into their house, and ministered to them all that was necessary and needful to them. Then as Mary Magdalene preached on a time, the said prince said to her: Weenest thou that thou mayst defend the law that thou preachest? And she answered: Certainly, I am ready to defend it, as she that is confirmed every day by miracles, and by the predication of our master, S. Peter, which now sitteth in the see at Rome. To whom then the prince said: I and my wife be ready to obey thee in all things, if thou mayst get of thy god whom thou preachest, that we might have a child. And then Mary Magdalene said that it should not be left, and then prayed unto our Lord that he would vouchsafe of his grace to give to them a son. And our Lord heard her prayers, and the lady conceived. Then her husband would go to S. Peter for to wit if it were true that Mary Magdalene had preached of Jesu Christ. Then his wife said to him: What will ye do sir, ween ye to go without me? Nay, when thou shalt depart, I shall depart with thee, and when thou shalt return again I shall return, and when thou shalt rest and tarry, I shall rest and tarry. To whom her husband answered, and said: Dame, it shall not be so, for thou art great, and the perils of the sea be without number. Thou mightest lightly perish, thou shalt abide at home and take heed to our possessions. And this lady for nothing would not change her purpose, but fell down on her knees at his feet sore weeping, requiring him to take her with him. And so at last he consented, and granted her request. Then Mary Magdalene set the sign of the cross on their shoulders, to the end that the fiend might not empesh ne let them in their journey. Then charged they a ship abundantly of all that was necessary to them, and left all their things in the keeping of Mary Magdalene, and went forth on their pilgrimage. And when they had made their course, and sailed a day and a night, there arose a great tempest and orage. And the wind increased and grew over hideous, in such wise that this lady, which was great, and nigh the time of her childing, began to wax feeble, and had great anguishes for the great waves and troubling of the sea, and soon after began to travail, and was delivered of a fair son, by occasion of the storm and tempest, and in her childing died. And when the child was born he cried for to have comfort of the teats of his mother, and made a piteous noise. Alas! what sorrow was this to the father, to have a son born which was the cause of the death of his mother, and he might not live, for there was none to nourish him. Alas! what shall this pilgrim do, that seeth his wife dead, and his son crying after the breast of his mother? And the pilgrim wept strongly and said: Alas! caitiff, alas! What shall I do? I desired to have a son, and I have lost both the mother and the son. And the mariners then said: This dead body must be cast mto the sea, or else we all shall perish, for as long as she shall abide with us, this tempest shall not cease. And when they had taken the body for to cast it into the sea, the husband said: Abide and suffer a little, and if ye will not spare to me my wife, yet at least spare the little child that cryeth, I pray you to tarry a while, for to know if the mother be aswoon of the pain, and that she might revive. And whilst he thus spake to them, the shipmen espied a mountain not far from the ship. And then they said that it was best to set the ship toward the land and to bury it there, and so to save it from devouring of the fishes of the sea. And the good man did so much with the mariners, what for prayers and for money, that they brought the body to the mountain. And when they should have digged for to make a pit to lay the body in, they found it so hard a rock that they might not enter for hardness of the stone. And they left the body there Iying, and covered it with a mantle; and the father laid his little son at the breast of the dead mother and said weeping: O Mary Magdalene, why camest thou to Marseilles to my great loss and evil adventure? Why have I at thine instance enterprised this journey? Hast thou required of God that my wife should conceive and should die at the childing of her son? For now it behoveth that the child that she hath conceived and borne, perish because it hath no nurse. This have I had by thy prayer, and to thee I commend them, to whom I have commended all my goods. And also I commend to thy God, if he be mighty, that he remember the soul of the mother, that he by thy prayer have pity on the child that he perish not. Then covered he the body all about with the mantle, and the child also, and then returned to the ship, and held forth his journey. And when he came to S. Peter, S. Peter came against him, and when he saw the sign of the cross upon his shoulder, he demanded him what he was, and wherefore he came, and he told to him all by order. To whom Peter said: Peace be to thee, thou art welcome, and hast believed good counsel. And be thou not heavy if thy wife sleep, and the little child rest with her, for our Lord is almighty for to give to whom he will, and to take away that he hath given, and to reestablish and give again that he hath taken, and to turn all heaviness and weeping into joy. Then Peter led him into Jerusalem, and showed to him all the places where Jesu Christ preached and did miracles, and the place where he suffered death, and where he ascended into heaven. And when he was well-informed of S. Peter in the faith, and that two years were passed sith he departed from Marseilles, he took his ship for to return again into his country. And as they sailed by the sea, they came, by the ordinance of God, by the rock where the body of his wife was left, and his son. Then by prayers and gifts he did so much that they arrived thereon. And the little child, whom Mary Magdalene had kept, went oft sithes to the seaside, and, like small children, took small stones and threw them into the sea. And when they came they saw the little child playing with stones on the seaside, as he was wont to do. And then they marvelled much what he was. And when the child saw them, which never had seen people tofore, he was afraid, and ran secretly to his mother's breast and hid him under the mantle. And then the father of the child went for to see more appertly, and took the mantle, and found the child, which was right fair, sucking his mother's breast. Then he took the child in his arms and said: O blessed Mary Magdalene, I were well happy and blessed if my wife were now alive, and might live, and come again with me into my country. I know verily and believe that thou who hast given to me my son, and hast fed and kept him two years in this rock, mayst well re-establish his mother to her first health. And with these words the woman respired, and took life, and said, like as she had been waked of her sleep: O blessed Mary Magdalene thou art of great merit and glorious, for in the pains of my deliverance thou wert my midwife, and in all my necessities thou hast accomplished to me the service of a chamberer. And when her husband heard that thing he amarvelled much, and said: Livest thou my right dear and best beloved wife? To whom she said: Yea, certainly I live, and am now first come from the pilgrimage from whence thou art come, and all in like wise as S. Peter led thee in Jerusalem, and showed to thee all the places where our Lord suffered death, was buried and ascended to heaven, and many other places, I was with you, with Mary Magdalene, which led and accompanied me, and showed to me all the places which I well remember and have in mind. And there recounted to him all the miracles that her husband had seen, and never failed of one article, ne went out of the way from the sooth. And then the good pilgrim received his wife and his child and went to ship. And soon after they came to the port of Marseilles. And they found the blessed Mary Magdalene preaching with her disciples. And then they kneeled down to her feet, and recounted to her all that had happened to them, and received baptism of S. Maximin. And then they destroyed all the temples of the idols in the city of Marseilles, and made churches of Jesu Christ. And with one accord they chose the blessed S. Lazarus for to be bishop of that city. And afterward they came to the city of Aix, and by great miracles and preaching they brought the people there to the faith of Jesu Christ. And there S. Maximin was ordained to be bishop. In this meanwhile the blessed Mary Magdalene, desirous of sovereign contemplation, sought a right sharp desert, and took a place which was ordained by the angel of God, and abode there by the space of thirty years without knowledge of anybody. In which place she had no comfort of running water, ne solace of trees, ne of herbs. And that was because our Redeemer did do show it openly, that he had ordained for her refection celestial, and no bodily meats. And every day at every hour canonical she was lifted up in the air of angels, and heard the glorious song of the heavenly companies with her bodily ears. Of which she was fed and filled with right sweet meats, and then was brought again by the angels unto her proper place, in such wise as she had no need of corporal nourishing. It happed that a priest, which desired to lead a solitary life, took a cell for himself a twelve-furlong from the place of Mary Magdalene. On a day our Lord opened the eyes of that priest, and he saw with his bodily eyes in what manner the angels descended into the place where the blessed Magdalene dwelt, and how they lifted her in the air, and after by the space of an hour brought her again with divine praisings to the same place. And then the priest desired greatly to know the truth of this marvellous vision, and made his prayers to Almighty God, and went with great devotion unto the place. And when he approached nigh to it a stone's cast, his thighs began to swell and wax feeble, and his entrails began within him to lack breath and sigh for fear. And as soon as he returned he had his thighs all whole, and ready for to go. And when he enforced him to go to the place, all his body was in languor, and might not move. And then he understood that it was a secret celestial place where no man human might come, and then he called the name of Jesu, and said: I conjure thee by our Lord, that if thou be a man or other creature reasonable, that dwellest in this cave, that thou answer me, and tell me the truth of thee. And when he had said this three times, the blessed Mary Magdalene answered: Come more near, and thou shalt know that thou desirest. And then he came trembling unto the half way, and she said to him: Rememberest thou not of the gospel of Mary Magdalene, the renowned sinful woman, which washed the feet of our Saviour with her tears, and dried them with the hair of her head, and desired to have forgiveness of her sins? And the priest said to her: I remember it well, that is more than thirty years that holy church believeth and confesseth that it was done. And then she said: I am she that by the space of thirty years have been here without witting of any person, and like as it was suffered to thee yesterday to see me, in like wise I am every day lift up by the hands of the angels into the air, and have deserved to hear with my bodily ears the right sweet song of the company celestial. And because it is showed to me of our Lord that I shall depart out of this world, go to Maximin, and say to him that the next day after the resurrection of our lord, in the same time that he is accustomed to arise and go to matins, that he alone enter into his oratory, and that by the ministry and service of angels he shall find me there. And the priest heard the voice of her, like as it had been the voice of an angel, but he saw nothing; and then anon he went to S. Maximin, and told to him all by order. Then S. Maximin was replenished of great joy, and thanked greatly our Lord. And on the said day and hour, as is aforesaid, he entered into his oratory, and saw the blessed Mary Magdalene standing in the quire or choir yet among the angels that brought her, and was lift up from the earth the space of two or three cubits. And praying to our Lord she held up her hands, and when S. Maximin saw her, he was afraid to approach to her. And she returned to him, and said: Come hither mine own father, and flee not thy daughter. And when he approached and came to her, as it is read in the books of the said S. Maximin, for the customable vision that she had of angels every day, the cheer and visage of her shone as clear as it had been the rays of the sun. And then all the clerks and the priests aforesaid were called, and Mary Magdalene received the body and blood of our Lord of the hands of the bishop with great abundance of tears, and after, she stretched her body tofore the altar, and her right blessed soul departed from the body and went to our Lord. And after it was departed, there issued out of the body an odour so sweet-smelling that it remained there by the space of seven days to all them that entered in. And the blessed Maximin anointed the body of her with divers precious ointments, and buried it honourably, and after commanded that his body should be buried by hers after his death.

Hegesippus, with other books of Josephus accord enough with the said story, and Josephus saith in his treatise that the blessed Mary Magdalene, after the ascension of our Lord, for the burning love that she had to Jesu Christ and for the grief and discomfort that she had for the absence of her master our Lord, she would never see man. But after when she came into the country of Aix, she went into desert, and dwelt there thirty years without knowing of any man or woman. And he saith that, every day at the seven hours canonical she was lifted in the air of the angels. But he saith that, when the priest came to her, he found her enclosed in her cell; and she required of him a vestment, and he delivered to her one, which she clothed and covered her with. And she went with him to the church and received the communion, and then made her prayers with joined hands, and rested in peace.

In the time of Charles the great, in the year of our Lord seven hundred and seventy-one, Gerard, duke of Burgundy might have no child by his wife, wherefore he gave largely alms to the poor people, and founded many churches, and many monasteries. And when he had made the abbey of Vesoul, he and the abbot of the monastery sent a monk with a good reasonable fellowship into Aix, for to bring thither if they might of the relics of S. Mary Magdalene. And when the monk came to the said city, he found it all destroyed of paynims. Then by adventure he found the sepulchre, for the writing upon the sepulchre of marble showed well that the blessed lady Mary Magdalene rested and lay there, and the history of her was marvellously entailed and carved in the sepulchre. And then this monk opened it by night and took the relics, and bare them to his lodging. And that same night Mary Magdalene appeared to that monk, saying: Doubt thee nothing, make an end of the work. Then he returned homeward until he came half a mile from the monastery. But he might in no wise remove the relics from thence, till that the abbot and monks came with procession, and received them honestly. And soon after the duke had a child by his wife.

There was a knight that had a custom every year to go a pilgrimage unto the body of S. Mary Magdalene, which knight was slain in battle. And as his friends wept for him lying on his bier, they said with sweet and devout quarrels, why she suffered her devout servant to die without confession and penance. Then suddenly he that was dead arose, all they being sore abashed, and made one to call a priest to him, and confessed him with great devotion, and received the blessed sacrament, and then rested in peace.

There was a ship charged with men and women that was perished and all to-brake, and there was among them a woman with child, which saw herself in peril to be drowned, and cried fast on Mary Magdalene for succour and help, making her avow that if she might be saved by her merits, and escape that peril, if she had a son she should give him to the monastery. And anon as she had so avowed, a woman of honourable habit and beauty appeared to her, and took her by the chin and brought her to the rivage all safe, and the other perished and were drowned. And after, she was delivered and had a son, and accomplished her avow like as she had promised.

Some say that S. Mary Magdalene was wedded to S. John the Evangelist when Christ called him from the wedding, and when he was called from her, she had thereof indignation that her husband was taken from her, and went and gave herself to all delight, but because it was not convenable that the calling of S. John should be occasion of her damnation, therefore our Lord converted her mercifully to penance, and because he had taken from her sovereign delight of the flesh, he replenished her with sovereign delight spiritual tofore all other, that is the love of God. And it is said that he ennobled S. John tofore all other with the sweetness of his familiarity, because he had taken him from the delight aforesaid.

There was a man which was blind on both his eyes, and did him to be led to the monastery of the blessed Mary Magdalene for to visit her body. His leader said to him that he saw the church. And then the blind man escried and said with a high voice: O blessed Mary Magdalene, help me that I may deserve once to see thy church. And anon his eyes were opened, and saw clearly all things about him.

There was another man that wrote his sins in a schedule and laid it under the coverture of the altar of Mary Magdalene, meekly praying her that she should get for him pardon and forgiveness, and a while after, he took the schedule again, and found all his sins effaced and struck out. Another man was holden in prison for debt of money, in irons. And he called unto his help ofttimes Mary Magdalene. And on a night a fair woman appeared to him and brake all his irons, and opened the door, and commanded him to go his way; and when he saw himself loose he fled away anon.

There was a clerk of Flanders named Stephen Rysen, and mounted in so great and disordinate felony, that he haunted all manner sins. And such thing as appertained to his health he would not hear. Nevertheless he had great devotion in the blessed Mary Magdalene and fasted her vigil, and honoured her feast. And on a time as he visited her tomb, he was not all asleep nor well awaked, when Mary Magdalene appeared to him like a much fair woman, sustained with two angels, one on the right side, and another on the left side, and said to him, looking on him despitously: Stephen, why reputest thou the deeds of my merits to be unworthy? Wherefore mayst not thou at the instance of my merits and prayers be moved to penance? For sith the time that thou begannest to have devotion in me, I have alway prayed God for thee firmly. Arise up therefore and repent thee, and I shall not leave thee till thou be reconciled to God. And then forthwith he felt so great grace shed in him, that he forsook and renounced the world and entered into religion, and was after of right perfect life. And at the death of him was seen Mary Magdalene, standing beside the bier with angels which bare the soul up to heaven with heavenly song in likeness of a white dove. Then let us pray to this blessed Mary Magdalene that she get us grace to do penance here for our sins, that after this life we may come to her in everlasting bliss in heaven. Amen.

Aurea Legenda: The Golden Legend or the Lives of the Saints by Jacobus de Voraigne, Archbishop of Genoa 1275, 1st Edition 1470, English by William Caxton, 1st Edition 1483, Edited by F. S. Ellis, Temple Classics, 1900 (reprint 1931).

Also

Internet Medieval Source Book, Fordham University Center for Medieval Studies.

Appendix E

Notes on Genealogies, Appendices E-J,

Arundel and Belvoir Documents and the Cartularies of Rouen

The Arundel and Belvoir documents are so called because they form the private collections kept in the respective castles of Arundel and Belvoir. Arundel Castle was started by Roger de Montgomery and part of the original Norman Tower still exists. When Robert de Montgomery of Bellême supported Robert of Normandy against Henry I for the throne of England, his lands in England were confiscated. Later, the castle came into the possession of the Despencer family, for whom the 2nd creation of Earl of Arundel was made and from whom the present FitzAlan Howard family of the Dukes of Norfolk descend. As it happens, the present Duchess of Norfolk descends from the Montgomery Earls of Eglinton, so when their son becomes Duke of Norfolk the castle will once more be back with a descendant of the original owners.

Belvoir castle was started by the de Toesny (various spellings) family and is the ancestral home of the Dukes of Rutland, who descend in a direct line from the original family. However, the present castle is the 4th to be built on this site, the original having been destroyed in the Wars of the Roses.

The earliest documents in these collections are a series of charters, marriage settlements and other documents which form the basis for a series of genealogies of the various families, which were related to or married to the Norman and Plantagenet dynasties.

In 1882 a barrister and Fellow of Emmanuel College, Cambridge, John Yeatman, used these documents to produce a book called *History of the House of Arundel*, published by Mitchell and Hughes of London. He was a very careful researcher and on each page, references the relevant document. He also went to France and carefully documented the *Cartularies of Rouen*, which sadly did not survive the 2nd World War.

145

We are therefore extremely lucky to have many of them documented in this history.

I have used them as the basis for many of the genealogies in this book.

In *The God-Kings of England* there is a mistake on pp. 145 & 146. The genealogies in this book were originally done in Windows 95. When upgrading to Windows XP I exported these genealogies, but many of the lines became muddled. In trying to correct them I did so without referring to my originals and some mistakes occurred. Hamon aux Dents descends from Malger or Mauger, Count of Mortain and Corbeil, not Mauger, Archbishop of Rouen. The remainder of page 146 is taken from the work of L.-A. de St. Clair (*Histoire Généalogique de la Famille de St. Clair et de ses Alliances*), about which I have considerable doubt.

The corrected genealogy follows:

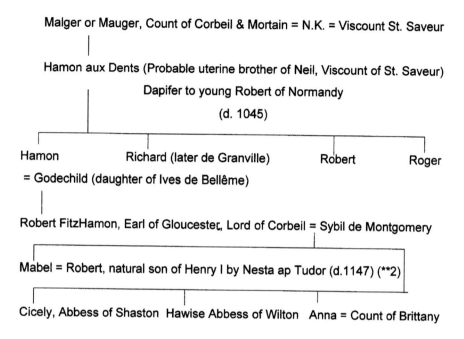

Malger or Mauger, Count of Corbeil & Mortain = N.K. = Viscount St. Saveur

Hamon aux Dents (Probable uterine brother of Neil, Viscount of St. Saveur)

Dapifer to young Robert of Normandy

(d. 1045)

Hamon   Richard (later de Granville)   Robert   Roger

= Godechild (daughter of Ives de Bellême)

Robert FitzHamon, Earl of Gloucester, Lord of Corbeil = Sybil de Montgomery

Mabel = Robert, natural son of Henry I by Nesta ap Tudor (d.1147) (**2)

Cicely, Abbess of Shaston Hawise Abbess of Wilton Anna = Count of Brittany

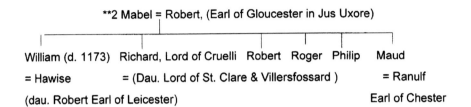

**2 Mabel = Robert, (Earl of Gloucester in Jus Uxore)

William (d. 1173)   Richard, Lord of Cruelli   Robert   Roger   Philip   Maud

= Hawise   = (Dau. Lord of St. Clare & Villersfossard)   = Ranulf

(dau. Robert Earl of Leicester)   Earl of Chester

The above genealogy is taken from transcripts of documents found at Wardour Castle and now in the Arundel Collection.

Appendix F

House of Giroie (1)

Abbo the Breton = ?

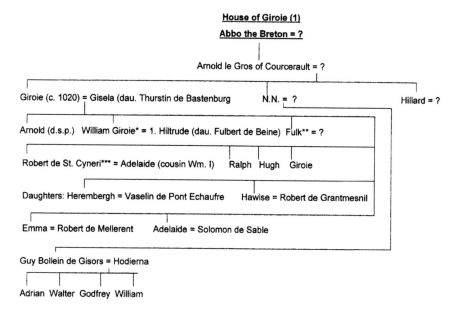

Arnold le Gros of Courcerault = ?

Giroie (c. 1020) = Gisela (dau. Thurstin de Bastenburg   N.N. = ?   Hillard = ?

Arnold (d.s.p.)   William Giroie* = 1. Hiltrude (dau. Fulbert de Beine)   Fulk** = ?

Robert de St. Cyneri*** = Adelaide (cousin Wm. I)   Ralph Hugh Giroie

Daughters: Herembergh = Vaselin de Pont Echaufre   Hawise = Robert de Grantmesnil

Emma = Robert de Mellerent   Adelaide = Solomon de Sable

Guy Bollein de Gisors = Hodierna

Adrian Walter Godfrey William

House of Giroie (2)

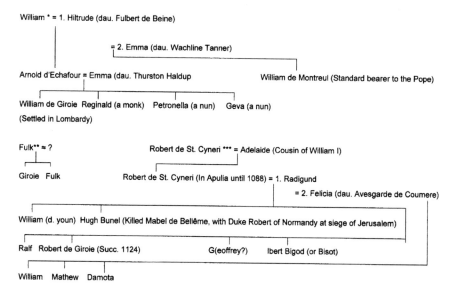

William * = 1. Hiltrude (dau. Fulbert de Beine)

= 2. Emma (dau. Wachline Tanner)

Arnold d'Echafour = Emma (dau. Thurston Haldup)   William de Montreul (Standard bearer to the Pope)

William de Giroie Reginald (a monk) Petronella (a nun) Geva (a nun)
(Settled in Lombardy)

Fulk** ≈ ?   Robert de St. Cyneri *** = Adelaide (Cousin of William I)

Giroie Fulk   Robert de St. Cyneri (In Apulia until 1088) = 1. Radigund

= 2. Felicia (dau. Avesgarde de Coumere)

William (d. youn) Hugh Bunel (Killed Mabel de Bellême, with Duke Robert of Normandy at siege of Jerusalem)

Ralf Robert de Giroie (Succ. 1124)   G(eoffrey?)   Ibert Bigod (or Bisot)

William Mathew Damota

References: Yeatman, J. (1882) – History of the House of Arundel, Mitchell & Hughes, London

Appendix G

House of Grantmesnil
Robert de Grantmesnil

(Family of Breton origin arrived Normandy at time of Richard II of Normandy - Killed in Battle by Roger de Beaumont 1035)

= Hawise (dau. Giroie d'Echafour & Montreul – See House of Giroie) =

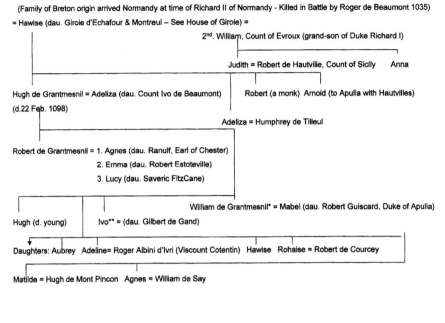

2nd. William, Count of Evroux (grand-son of Duke Richard I)

Judith = Robert de Hautville, Count of Sicily   Anna

Hugh de Grantmesnil = Adeliza (dau. Count Ivo de Beaumont)   Robert (a monk) Arnold (to Apulia with Hautvilles)

(d.22 Feb. 1098)

Adeliza = Humphrey de Tilleul

Robert de Grantmesnil = 1. Agnes (dau. Ranulf, Earl of Chester)

2. Emma (dau. Robert Estoteville)

3. Lucy (dau. Saveric FitzCane)

William de Grantmesnil* = Mabel (dau. Robert Guiscard, Duke of Apulia)

Hugh (d. young)   Ivo** = (dau. Gilbert de Gand)

Daughters: Aubrey Adeline= Roger Albini d'Ivri (Viscount Cotentin) Hawise Rohaise = Robert de Courcey

Matilde = Hugh de Mont Pincon Agnes = William de Say

House of Grantmesnil (2)

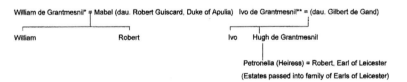

William de Grantmesnil* = Mabel (dau. Robert Guiscard, Duke of Apulia) Ivo de Grantmesnil** = (dau. Gilbert de Gand)

William   Robert   Ivo   Hugh de Grantmesnil

Petronella (Heiress) = Robert, Earl of Leicester

(Estates passed into family of Earls of Leicester)

Appendix H

House of Bayeaux and St. Saveur

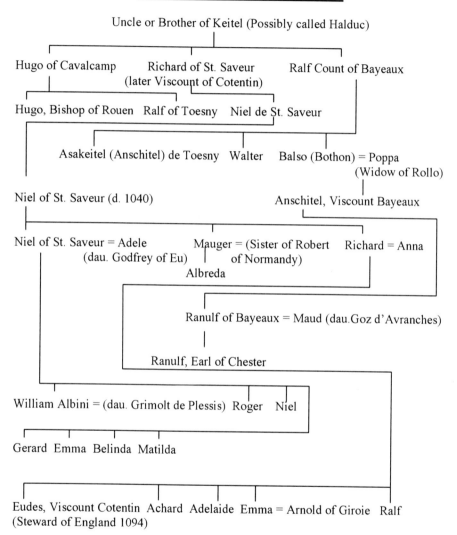

Uncle or Brother of Keitel (Possibly called Halduc)

Hugo of Cavalcamp   Richard of St. Saveur   Ralf Count of Bayeaux
(later Viscount of Cotentin)

Hugo, Bishop of Rouen   Ralf of Toesny   Niel de St. Saveur

Asakeitel (Anschitel) de Toesny   Walter   Balso (Bothon) = Poppa
(Widow of Rollo)

Niel of St. Saveur (d. 1040)   Anschitel, Viscount Bayeaux

Niel of St. Saveur = Adele   Mauger = (Sister of Robert   Richard = Anna
(dau. Godfrey of Eu)   of Normandy)
Albreda

Ranulf of Bayeaux = Maud (dau. Goz d'Avranches)

Ranulf, Earl of Chester

William Albini = (dau. Grimolt de Plessis)   Roger   Niel

Gerard Emma Belinda Matilda

Eudes, Viscount Cotentin Achard Adelaide Emma = Arnold of Giroie Ralf
(Steward of England 1094)

Appendix I

Robert Beaumels (Uncle of Roger de Montgomery)

(created Lord of Ashby 1068)

|

Richard Belmeis (Change of spelling)

(Dapifer to Roger de Montgomery, Earl of Shrewsbury)

= Constance, (dau. King William I)

Richard de Belmeis (Bishop of london)   Walter, Lord of Asby & Salop = Aveline   daughter

Richard (Bishop of london)   Philip of Ashby & Salop = Matilde (dau. William de Meschines)   Robert

Rainulf (dsp 1167)   Philip (dsp 1159)   Adeline (heiress) = Alan le Zouch, Viscount de Rohan

William de la Zoiuch (took name of Belmeis)   Roger de la Zouch

↓

Had Issue

152

Appendix J

House of Toesny or Toeni

Uncle of Rollo of Normandy

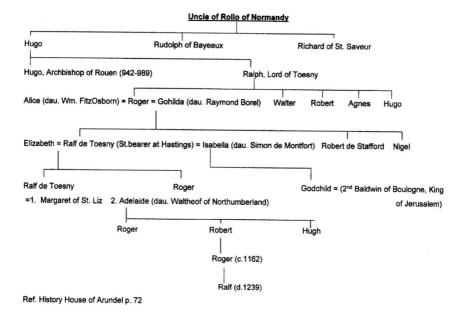

Hugo   Rudolph of Bayeaux   Richard of St. Saveur

Hugo, Archbishop of Rouen (942-989)   Ralph, Lord of Toesny

Alice (dau. Wm. FitzOsborn) = Roger = Gohilda (dau. Raymond Borel)   Walter   Robert   Agnes   Hugo

Elizabeth = Ralf de Toesny (St.bearer at Hastings) = Isabella (dau. Simon de Montfort)   Robert de Stafford   Nigel

Ralf de Toesny   Roger   Godchild = (2nd Baldwin of Boulogne, King
=1. Margaret of St. Liz   2. Adelaide (dau. Waltheof of Northumberland)   of Jerusalem)

Roger   Robert   Hugh

Roger (c.1162)

Ralf (d.1239)

Ref. History House of Arundel p. 72

153

Appendix K

Ulvungar Counts of Aversa and Princes of Capua

Rainulf I (Drengot) – Count of Aversa (1030-1045)
Asclettin I (Nephew) – Count of Aversa (1045-1058)
Richard I – Count of Aversa and first Norman Prince of Capua (1058-1078)
Jordan I – Prince of Capua (1078-1091)
Richard II – Prince of Capua (1091-1106)
(Lando IV held Capua in opposition to Richard II 1092-1098)
Robert I – Prince of Capua (1106-1120)
Richard III – Prince of Capua (1120)
Jordan II – Prince of Capua (1120-1127)
Robert II – Prince of Capua (1127-1156)
(Alfonso held as fief of Roger II of Sicily 1135-1144)
(William held as fief of Roger II of Sicily 1144-1154)

From 1156 onwards it becomes an appendage of the Kingdom of Sicily for 2nd sons:
Robert III (1155-1158)
Henry I (1166-1172)

Appendix L

Kings of Jerusalem

1099-1100 – Godfrey (Protector of the Holy Sepulchre)
1100-1118 – Baldwin I
1118-1131 – Baldwin II
1131-1153 – Melisende & Fulk
1143-1162 – Baldwin III (co-crown with Melisende until 1153)
1162-1174 – Amalric I
1174-1185 – Baldwin IV
1185-1186 – Baldwin V
1186-1187 – Sibylla & Guy

Jerusalem was lost in 1187 but Kingdom continued at Acre until 1291.

Appendix M

Counts and Kings of Sicily

Sicily was granted to Robert Guiscard as a Dukedom in 1059 by Pope Nicholas II. Guiscard in turn granted it to his brother Roger as a County.

Counts of Sicily

1071-1101 – Roger I
1101-1105 – Simon
1105-1130 – Roger II

Kings of Sicily

Roger I received royal investiture from the Antipope Anacletus II in 1130 and full recognition from Pope Innocent II in 1139. The kingdom now consisted of not only the Island, but also the southern third of Italy, plus Malta and the Mahdia in North Africa.

1130-1154 – Roger II
1154-1166 – William I
1166-1189 – William II
1189-1194 – Tancred
1194 – William III
1194-1198 – Constance = The Emperor Henry VI
1198-1250 – Frederick I (also Holy Roman Emperor)
1250-1254 – Conrad I (also German King)
1254-1258 – Conrad II (Conradin of Swabia)
1258-1266 – Manfred

Appendix N

The Teutonic Knights Grand Masters

Early Masters

1190-1192 – Sibrand (Meister)
1192-1193 – Gerhard
1193-1195 – Heinrich (Prior)
1195-1196 – Ulrich
1196-1198 – Heinrich Walpot von Bassenheim (Preceptor)

Grand Masters

1198-1200 – Heinrich Walpot von Bassenheim (Grand Master)
1200-1208 – Otto von Kerpen
1208-1209 – Heinrich von Tunna
1209-1239 – Hermann von Salza
1239-1240 – Conrad von Thuringia
1240-1244 – Gerhard von Malberg
1244-1249 – Heinrich von Hohenlohe
1249-1252 – Günther von Wüllersleben
1252-1256 – Poppo von Osterna
1256-1273 – Anno von Sangershausen
1273-1282 – Hartmann von Heldrugen
1282(1283)-1290 – Burchard von Schwanden
1290-1297 – Konrad von Feuchtwangen
1297-1303 – Gottfried von Hohenlohe
1303-1311 – Siegfried von Feuchtwangen

1311-1324 – Karl von Trier
1324-1330 – Werner von Orseln
1331-1335 – Luther von Braunschweig
1335-1341 – Dietrich von Altenburg
1342-1345 – Ludolf König
1345-1351 – Heinrich Dusemer
1351-1382 – Winrich von Kniprode
1382-1390 – Conrad Zöllner von Rothenstein
1391-1393 – Konrad von Wallenrode
1393-1407 – Konrad von Jungingen
1407-1410 – Ulrich von Jungingen
1410-1413 – Heinrich von Plauen
1414-1422 – Michael Küchmeister von Sternberg
1422-1441 – Paul von Rusdorf
1441-1449 – Konrad von Erlichshausen
1449(1450)-1467 – Ludwig von Erlichshausen
1467-1470 – Heinrich Reuss von Plauen
1470-1477 – Heinrich von Richtenburg
1477-1489 – Martin von Wetzhausen
1489-1497 – Johann von Tiefen
1497-1510 – Frederick von Saxony
1510-1525 – Albert von Brandenburg-Ansbach (Albert of Prussia)

Appendix O

Grand Masters of the Knights Templar

1118-1136 – Hughes de Payens
1136-1147 – Robert de Craon
1147-1149 – Everard des Barres
1149-1153 – Bernard de Tremelay
1153-1156 – André de Montbard
1156-1169 – Bertrand de Blanchefort
1169-1171 – Philippe de Milly
1171-1179 – Odo de St. Amand
1179-1181 – No Grand Master
1181-1184 – Arnold de Torroja
1184-1189 – Gérard de Ridefort
1189-1191 – No Grand Master
1191-1193 – Robert de Sablé
1193-1200 – Gilbert Horal
1201-1208 – Phillipe de Plessis
1209-1219 – Guillaume de Chartres
1218(1219)-1232 – Pedro de Montaigu
1232-1244 – Armand de Périgord
1244-1247 – Richard de Bures (*Disputed*)
1247-1250 – Guillaume de Sonnac
1250-1256 – Renaud de Vichiers
1256-1273 – Thomas Bérard
1273-1291 – Guillaume de Beaujeu
1291-1292 – Thibaud Gaudin
1292-1314 – Jacques de Molay

Appendix P

Names of the Exilarchs of the Jews in Babylon

King Evil-Merodach, Ruler of Babylon (562-560 BC) elevated Jehoiachin, the exiled King of the Jews, to the position of Ruler of all Jews in his domains. This Exilarchy ruled from their own Palace in Babylon until 1401, when they transferred to Baghdad where they continued to rule until 1700. Cyrus II (538-530 BC) allowed Zarrubabel, another Davidic descendant, to return to Jerusalem. There are therefore three lines of Davidic descent: the line of the Exilarchs, which was undoubtedly the senior line, the line of Zerrubabel from whom Jesus descended, and the line of the Exilarchs of the West, represented by the Nasis or Makirs of Septimania.

The following is a list of Exilarchs from about the year 500 AD until about 700 AD:

Abba
Barachiai
Hananai I
Hananai II
Hasadiai
Huna I
Huna II
Huna III
Huna IV (Mar) (Sometimes called Huna Mar I)
Huna V
Huna VI
Jesiai
Kahana I
Kahana II
Mar Ukba I
Mar Ukba II

Mar Zutra I
Nahum
Nathan I
Nathan II
Nehemiah
Obadiai
Salathiel
Shemaiai
Hisdai Shahrijar
Bustanai ben Haninai **
Haninai Bar Adoi

** From here descend the Makirs of Septimania

Appendix Q

Counts of Anjou

870-898 – Ingelger
898-941 – Fulk I
941-958 – Fulk II
958-987 – Geoffrey I
987-1040 – Fulk III (Nerra)
1040-1060 – Geoffrey II (Martel)
1060-1067 – Geoffrey III
1067-1109 – Fulk IV
1098-1106 – Geoffrey IV (co-ruler)
1106-1129 – Fulk V (later King of Jerusalem)
1129-1151 – Geoffrey V (Plantagenet)
1151-1189 – Henry I (also King of England as Henry II)
1170-1183 – Henry II (co-ruler)
1189-1199 – Richard I (also King of England)
1199-1203 – Arthur I

In 1204 Anjou became an apanage of the French Crown.

Appendix R

COUNTS OF TOULOUSE
(HOUSE OF ROUERGUE)

844-852 – FREDELON
844-849 – WILLIAM (Opposed Fredelon)
852-863 – RAYMOND
863-865 – HUMFRID (deposed Raymond)
863-865 – SUNIFRED (Opposed Humfrid)
865-877 – BERNARD
877-886 – BERNARD
886-918 – ODO
918-924 – RAYMOND
924-950 – RAYMOND PONS
950-961 – RAYMOND
961-972 – HUGH
972-978 – RAYMOND
978-1037 – WILLIAM
1037-1061 – PONS
1061-1094 – WILLIAM
1094-1095 – RAYMOND (called IV)
1095-1112 – BERTRAND
1119-1148 – ALFONSO JORDAN
1148-1194 – RAYMOND
1194-1222 – RAYMOND
1222-1249 – RAYMOND

1249-1271 – JOAN (In her own right) = Alfonso de Poitou
Toulouse passes to French Crown under the Treaty of Languedoc.

There are probably between 1-3 missing names of Counts.

Appendix S

Kassite Dynasty of Babylon

c. 1600 BC – Gandash

– ?

c. 1570 BC – Agum I

c. 1510 BC – Burnah-Buriash I

c. 1490 BC – Kashtiliashu III

– ?

c. 1465 BC – Agum III

c. 1415 – Kara-Indash

c. 1400 – Kadashman-Harbe I

c. 1390 – Kurigalzu I

c. 1370 – Kadashman-Enlil I

c. 1350 – Burnah-Bariash II

1350-1345 – Kara-Hardash & Nazi-Burgash

1345-1324 BC – Kurigalzu II

1324-1298 BC – Nazi-Murattash

1298-1280 BC – Kadashman-Turgu

1280-1265 BC – Kadashman-Enlil II

1265-1256 BC – Kudur-Enlil

1256-1243 BC – Shagarakti-Shuriash

1243-1235 BC – Kashtiliashu IV

1235-1228 BC – **Interregnum**

1228-1225 BC – Enlil-nadin-shumi & Kadashman-Harbe III

1225-1219 BC – Adad-Shuma-Iddina (the first Odin)

1219-1189 BC – Adad-Shumar-usur

1189-1174 BC – Meli-Shipak

1174-1161 BC – Marduk-Apla-Iddina

1161-1160 BC – Zababa-Shumar-Iddina

1160-1157 BC – Enlil-Nadin-Ahi

End of Kassite Dynasty and beginning of 2nd Isin Dynasty.

__Appendix T (1)__

THE GENEALOGY OF THE KINGS OF THE
EAST-ANGLES.

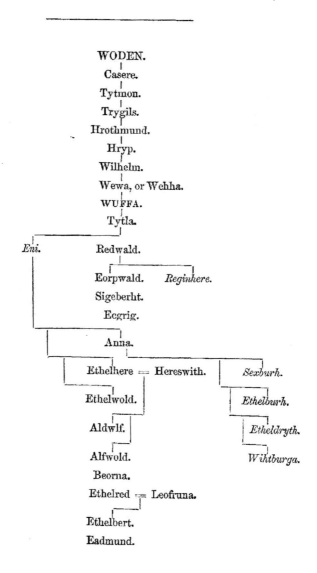

WODEN.

Casere.

Tytmon.

Trygils.

Hrothmund.

Hryp.

Wilhelm.

Wewa, or Wehha.

WUFFA.

Tytla.

Eni.   Redwald.

Eorpwald.   *Reginhere.*

Sigeberht.

Ecgrig.

Anna.

Ethelhere ═ Hereswith.   *Sexburh.*

Ethelwold.   *Ethelburh.*

Aldwlf.   *Etheldryth.*

Alfwold.   *Wihtburga.*

Beorna.

Ethelred ═ Leofruna.

Ethelbert.

Eadmund.

Appendix T (2)

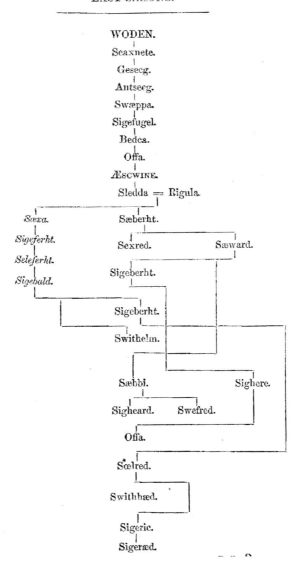

Appendix T (3)

THE GENEALOGY OF THE KINGS OF KENT.

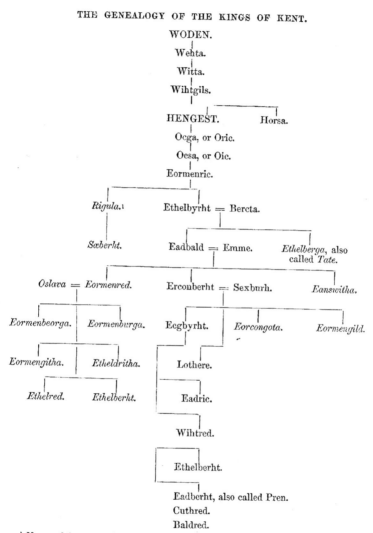

WODEN.

Wehta.

Witta.

Wihtgils.

HENGEST.　　Horsa.

Ocga, or Oric.

Oesa, or Oic.

Eormenric.

Rigula.[1]　　Ethelbyrht = Bercta.

Sæberht.　　Eadbald = Emme.　　*Ethelberga,* also called *Tate.*

Oslava = *Eormenred.*　　Erconberht = Sexburh.　　*Eanswitha.*

Eormenbeorga.　　*Eormenburga.*　　Ecgbyrht.　　*Eorcongota.*　　*Eormengild.*

Eormengitha.　　*Etheldritha.*　　Lothere.

Ethelred.　　*Ethelberht.*　　Eadric.

Wihtred.

Ethelberht.

Eadberht, also called Pren.

Cuthred.

Baldred.

[1] Names of the younger branches are printed in *italics*, to distinguish them from the kings and queens.

<u>Appendix T (4)</u>

THE GENEALOGY OF THE KINGS OF THE LINDISFARI.

WODEN.
|
Winta.
|
Cretta.
|
Queldgils.
|
Cædbæd.
|
Bubba.
|
Beda.
|
Biscop.
|
Eangferth.
|
Eatta.
|
Ealdfrith.

<u>Appendix T (5:i)</u>
<u>Kings of Mercia</u>
Woden

Weolthelgeat

Waga

Wihtlaeg

Vermund

Offa
Angengeat*

Eomer

Icil

Cnebba

Cynewald

Creodda

Pybba

* Not mentioned in Beowulf

Appendix T (5:ii)

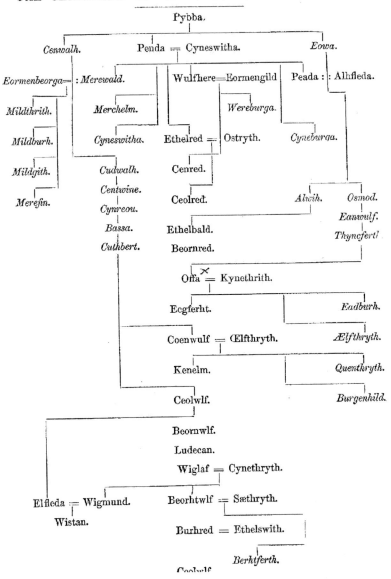

Appendix T (6)

Northumbrian Kings 1

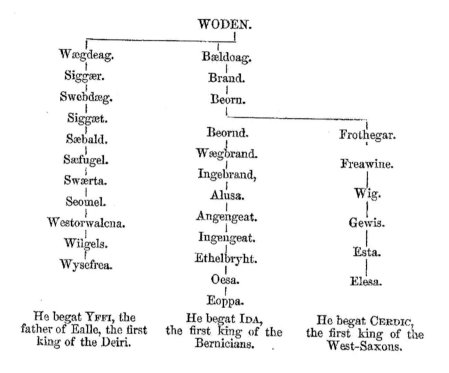

WODEN.

Wægdeag.	Bældoag.	
Siggær.	Brand.	
Swebdæg.	Beorn.	
Siggæt.		
Sæbald.	Beornd.	Frothegar.
Sæfugel.	Wægbrand.	Freawine.
Swærta.	Ingebrand,	
Seomel.	Alusa.	Wig.
Westorwalcna.	Angengeat.	Gewis.
Wilgels.	Ingengeat.	Esta.
Wysefrea.	Ethelbryht.	Elesa.
	Oesa.	
	Eoppa.	

He begat YFFI, the father of Ealle, the first king of the Deiri.

He begat IDA, the first king of the Bernicians.

He begat CERDIC, the first king of the West-Saxons.

THE GENEALOGY OF THE KINGS OF NORTHUMBRIA.—Continued.

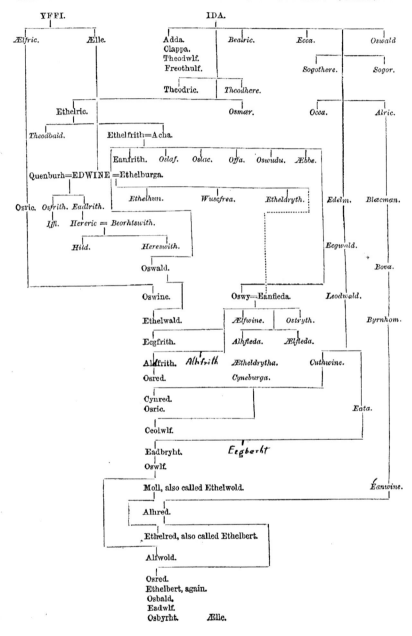

YFFI.

IDA.

Ælfric.   Ælle.

Adda.
Clappa.
Theodwlf.
Freothulf.

Bealric.

Ecca.

Oswald

Sogothere.

Sogor.

Theodric.   *Theodhere.*

Ethelric.

Osmær.

Occa.

Alric.

Theodbald.

Ethelfrith=Acha.

Eanfrith.   *Oslaf.   Oslac.   Offa.   Oswudu.   Æbbe.*

Quenburh=EDWINE=Ethelburga.

Ethelhun.   *Wuscfrea.*   *Etheldryth.*   *Edelm.*   *Blæcman.*

Osric. *Osfrith. Eadrith.*

Iffi.   Hereric = *Beorhtswith.*

Ecgwald.

Hild.   *Hereswith.*

Bova.

Oswald.

Oswine.

Oswy=Eanfleda.   *Leodwald.*

Ethelwald.

Ælfwine.   Ostryth.   *Byrnhom.*

Ecgfrith.

Alhfleda.   Ælfleda.

Alhfrith.   *Alhfrith*   *Ætheldrytha.*   *Cuthwine.*

Osred.

Cyneburga.

Cynred.
Osric.

Eata.

Ceolwlf.

Eadbryht.   *Eegberht*

Oswlf.

Moll, also called Ethelwold.   *Eanwine.*

Alhred.

Ethelred, also called Ethelbert.

Alfwold.

Osred.
Ethelbert, again.
Osbald.
Eadwlf.
Osbyrht.   Ælle.

Appendix U

Comments and References on the Peveral and Pagen (Payen) Genealogies

Hugh de Payen as founder of the Knights Templar is only mentioned by William of Tyre, in *Rerum in Partibus Transmarinis Gestarum* (written c. 1200) and in *Die lateinische Fortsetzung XII, 7*, pp. 520-521 and it is from this that we learn that Hugh was a knight of Champagne. But William himself wrote nearly one hundred years after the events took place. William was born in Jerusalem in 1130. In the Latin version the name is Pagano; in the German von Pagan, but there was a French translation which was widely circulated in the Middle Ages in which Hugh becomes Hughes de Payen. Odericus Vitalis, writing in Latin, calls him "Pagano" or "Paganis" (genitive). Sir Steven Runciman used the German version as well as the French and Latin versions in his work, *The History of the Crusades*, but I do not think was particularly bothered about Hugh's ancestors, so simply used "Hugh de Payen" and most historians have followed suit. The problem for us is, was he "de Payen" or "de Pagan," or was he originally called FitzPayen, son of Payen, from the habit of medieval writers to write the Latin Filius as "Flz."

On various internet sites there is a so-called genealogy for Hugh based upon the work of one Henri Lobineau and deposited in the Bibliotéque Nationale in the 1950's. This document is a complete fabrication. It came from a book by Michael Baigent, et al, called *Holy Blood, Holy Grail* and can be found on page 442 of the paperback edition.

It states that Hugh's father and grandfather were called Tibaud and that an aunt married Hughes de Chaumont who is said to be the Lord of Gisors. This is a load of rubbish! Guy Bollein was lord of Gisors at that time; furthermore he had four sons, one of whom became Lord of Gisors after him and from whom descended Jean de Gisors, the founder of Portsmouth in England.

I suggest that in fact Hugh descends from a very distinguished line of Welsh princes, whose grandfather, called Ranulf Peveral in the Norman chronicles, and was also called Ranulf or Ralf ap Rhys in the Cymric border documents. His grandfather, Ranulf, had married for a second time, late in life, the ex-mistress of William I and Ranulf's niece Nesta, would become the mistress of Henry I, William's youngest son. Like father, like son.

The name Peveral was not a surname, but a nickname or cognomen from Pevr, meaning "Fair." The Normans often used nicknames (see *The God-Kings of England*, pp. 104-115). However William I's illegitimate son adopted his step-father's cognomen as a surname and the illegitimate branch became known as Peveral. The Norman's Latinised it as Piperellus, from the Latin verb "pipio," meaning to cheep or peep (as in young birds). We would say "pipsqueak" in modern English and it had much the same connotation.

The elder branch of the family eventually adopted their original title as Princes of Powis, as their surname, and became known as Powis, or sometimes Poles (de Powis or de Poles).

Hugh's father, Pagan, was known as Pagan Peveral, in some chronicles he is called Pain Peveral or Payen Peveral, and became Robert of Normandy's Standard Bearer during the 1st Crusade. Indeed Pagan had moved to Normandy in the service of the Dukes and when his son was old enough, Pagan probably sent him to the Court in Champagne to learn to become a Knight. This was normal practice amongst the French and Norman aristocracy (see Duane, O. B. – *Chivalry*, p. 45). Here he was known as fitzPagan or fitzPayen (son of Pagan). Whether Hugh was part of the initial crusade or whether he went later is unknown, but when his father died fighting, he probably regarded it as his duty to follow in his father's footsteps. This was probably how many of second wave of knights finished up in Edessa.

It has always seemed strange to me that an unknown Champagnois knight could suddenly form the Knights Templar, but the descendant of the Princes of Powis and, by marriage, related to the great Houses of Normandy and Montgomery was quite another matter.

It also explains the somewhat curious statement of Odericus (917) when mentioning Hugh Paganis and which in turn is mentioned in

Domesday, regarding the manors of Oswestry, Wittingham and Cherbury, manors which changed hands regularly between the Princes of Powis and the English. "Tempore Regis Adelredi patris Edwardi Regis reddebant haec tria Maneria dimidiam firmam noctis."

Indeed, Hugh's family would have owned them prior to Ethelred and the manors obviously reverted to the Princes of Powis at the time of Edward the Confessor.

References:
Appendix U

1. *The Cartularies of Rouen* (*Cart de Normandie* MSS), of which I have a 19th century English translation, state that a Hughes fitzPain married a Catherine de Chaumont. They do not, of course, state that he later became Grand Master of Templars.

2. The list of knights who accompanied Robert of Normandy call Robert's standard bearer Pain Peveral.

3. A will of a Grand Master, which is assumed to be Hugh's by the date, but does not mention Hugh's surname, makes provision for his wife Elizabeth, but does not give her unmarried name. I have suggested de Vezny or Vesey and this seems born out by the coat-of-arms subsequently adopted by the Vesey family.

4. Peveral name and Pevr references come from the Arundel documents and the Cymric border documents.

5. Robert, Earl of Gloucester, was the natural son of Henry I and Nesta ap Tudor. He married Mabel, the daughter of Robert FitzHamon and Sybil de Montgomery. This is another example of a name change from Corbeil via Hamon-aux-dents to FitzHamon and de Hamon.

6. Chartulary of Plympton Priory (1121) contains an enormous amount of information on the FitzPains and their relatives. Mostly Payen is spelt Pain.

7. The legitimate family of Powis also became known as de Poles (26 Henry II).

The Peveral and Pagan (Payen) Families

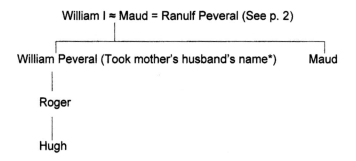

William I ≈ Maud = Ranulf Peveral (See p. 2)

William Peveral (Took mother's husband's name*)   Maud

Roger

Hugh

* Peveral is actually a Cognomen from Pevr meaning fair or beautiful. The Normans Latinised it as Piperellus.

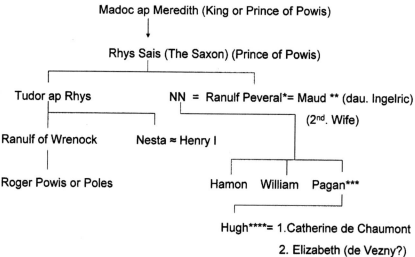

Madoc ap Meredith (King or Prince of Powis)

Rhys Sais (The Saxon) (Prince of Powis)

Tudor ap Rhys   NN = Ranulf Peveral*= Maud ** (dau. Ingelric)

                                    (2nd. Wife)

Ranulf of Wrenock   Nesta ≈ Henry I

Roger Powis or Poles   Hamon   William Pagan***

                                Hugh****= 1.Catherine de Chaumont

                                       2. Elizabeth (de Vezny?)

* Ranulf was an old man when he took as his 2nd. Wife Maud, the ex-mistress of William I. ** Maud's father was called Ingelric the Saxon. Ingelric is a name found in the Royal House of Wessex (West-Saxons). *** Pagan was the Standard Bearer to Robert of Normandy on the 1st Crusade and his son Hugh**** was called FitzPagan or FitzPayen or de Payen.

Vesey

REFERENCES, SOURCES & FURTHER READING

www.art.man.ac.uj/ARTHIST/Estates/Hamilton.htm
www.ancientroute.com/empire/edom.htm
http://www.bible.ca/history/fathers/ANF-08/anf08-66.htm
http://i-cias.com/e.o/nabateans.htm
http://www.earlybritishkingdoms.com/articles/josanc.html
http://www.domainofman.com/book/sup5.html
http://fmg.ac/Projects/MedLands/TOULOUSE.htm
http://www.touregypt.net/featurestories/set.htm

Abecassis, A. & Eisenberg, J. (1978) – *A Bible Ouverte*, Albin
Michel, Paris.
Abdias Manuscript, Norris Collection, USA.
Ackroyd, P. (2001) – *London*, Vintage Books.
Acts of Thomas, New Testament Apocrypha.
Al-Makkari, A. ibn M. (1968) – *History of the Mohammedan
Dynasties in Spain*, Editiones Espagnoles, Spain.
Albert of Aix (c. 1100) – *Liber Christianae Expeditionis pro
Ereptione Emundatione et Restitutione Sanctae Hierosolymitanae
Ecclesiae*, vols. I-III.
Albright, W. F. (1942) – *King Joiachim in Exile*, The Biblical
Archaeologist, UK.
Amatus of Montecassino – *Storia de'Normanni*, ed. Bartholomaeis,
(trans. J. J. Norwich).
Annals of the Kingdom of Ireland by the Four Masters, (trans.
O'Donovan – 1887-1901), Dublin.
Ante-Nicene Fathers, Vols. I-VIII, von Tischendorf Collection,
Strathclyde University Library.
Army Essays (2007) – *The Wends 580-1218 AD*, III-1a, DBA
Resources.
Ashley, M. (1973) – *The Life and Times of William I*, Weidenfeld &
Nicholson, UK.

Baigent, M. (2006) – *The Jesus Papers*, Harper-Element.
Bain, R. (1938) – *The Clans and Tartans of Scotland*, (7th edition),
W. Collins & Sons.
Baker, J. H. (1981) – *An Introduction to English Legal History*, 2nd

Edition, Butterworth & Co. London.

Barber, R. (1970) – *The Knight and Chivalry*, Longman, London.

Barber, R. (1978) – *Edward, Prince of Wales and Aquitaine*, Boydell Press.

Bartlett, R. (2000) – *England under the Norman and Angevin Kings 1075-1225*, Clarendon Press, UK.

Bauer, W. (1934) (English Edition – 1971) – *Orthodoxy and Heresy in Earliest Christianity*.

Bayeaux Tapestry, from photographs taken by Mr. E. Barrow.

Begg, E. (2000) – *The Cult of the Black Madonna*.

Bennett, M. (1988) – *Wace and Warfare*, Anglo-Norman Studies.

Bernard of Clairvaux (1129) – *De Laude Novae Militae*, Paris.

Bethany, House of (c.1420) – *Liber Burgundiorum*, Brussels (Private Collection).

Blondel, S. (1978) – *The Varangians of Byzantium*, (trans. Benedikz, B. S.), Cambridge.

Bradbury, J. (1998) – *The Battle of Hastings*, Sutton Publishing Ltd. UK.

Brown, D. (2000) – *Ring Gives Clue to Last Romans*, Journal of the Council of British Archaeology.

Brown, R. A. (1984) – *The Normans*, Boydell Press.

Campbell, J. (2000) – *The Anglo-Saxon State*, Hambledon & London, UK.

Canon, J. & Griffiths, R. (1988) – *Oxford History of the British Monarchy*, Oxford University Press.

Castledon, R. (1994) – *World History, A Chronological Dictionary of Dates*, Paragon, UK.

Chahiers Percherons, (1976) – No. 51, Assoc. de Amis du Perche, France.

Chron. Fontaneille, Library in Perche, France.

Clough, S. B. & Cole, C.W. (1967) – *Economic History of Europe*, Heath & Co. Boston.

Codex Petropolitanus, Liber Historiae Francorum.

Codex Theodosianus (315) – Edition Mommsen & Meyer.

Collection Cornelius Harmsfort, (1546-1627), Danish State Archives.

Comnena, A. (c. 1100) – *Alexiad* (ed. B. Leib) Vols I-III, Collection Byzantine de l'Association Guillaume Budé, Paris (1937-1945).
Crouch, D. (2002) – *The Normans*, Hambledon & London, UK.

Daud, ibn A. (1160-1161) – *Sefer Seder haKabbalah*, Adler's Manuscript No. 2237, Jewish Theological Seminary of America, USA.
David, C. W. (1920) – *Robert Curthose*, Harvard University Press.
Davis, N. (1999) – *The Isles: A History*, Macmillan, London, UK.
Dennys, R. (1987) – *Our Royal Sovereigns*, Danbury, UK.
Den Store Danske Encyklopaedi (1998).
De Voraign, Jacobus (1275) – *Aurea Legenda*, Edited by Ellis, F. S. (1900), Temple Classics, UK.
Dimont, M. J. (1962) – *Jews, God & History*, Signet Books, London, UK.
Domesday Book, (1985) Edition Hutchinson Ltd.
Drower, Lady E. S. (1937) – *The Mandeans of Iraq and Iran*, Oxford. Univ. Press.
Duane, O. B. (1997) – *Chivalry*, Brockhampton Press, UK.
Dudo of St. Quentin (c. 1025) – *De moribus et actis primorum Normanniae Ducum* (ed. J. Lair 1865), Caen.

Eisenmann, R & Wise, M. (1992) – *The Dead Sea Scrolls Uncovered*, Penguin Books.
Eisenmann, R. (1977) – *James the Brother of Jesus*, Viking Penguin.
Encyclopaedia Britannica, 11th Edition.
Eusebius, (1981) – *History of the Church from Christ to Constantine*, (translated by G. A. Williamson), Harmondsworth. Also (1998 reprint), Hendrickson Publishers Inc., MA.
Eusebius of Caesarea, (c. 325 AD) – *Epistle of Jesus Christ to Abgarus, King of Edessa*, Harmondsworth.

Florence of Worchester, Manuscript published in 1854 by Henry Bohn, partly translated by Thomas Forrester, Djursholm, Sweden.
Ford, D. N. (2006) – *Early British Kingdoms*, Articles josanc.
Fulcher of Chartres – *Gesta Francorum Iherusalem Peregrinantium*, (ed. Hagenmeyer 1913), Heidelberg.

Gardiner, G. (2000) – *The Bloodline of the Holy Grail.*

Garrett, G. (1988) – *Conquered England 1066-1215*, Oxford Illustrated History of Medieval Europe, UK.

Gesta Danorum, Books 1-10, Danish State Archives.

Gillingham, J. (1998) – *The Normans in the Lives of the Kings and Queens of England*, Weidenfeld and Nicholson Ltd. UK.

Glueck, N. (1965) – *Deities and Dolphins: The Story of the Nabataeans*, New York.

Guy de Amiens, (c.1100) – *Carmen de Hastingae Proelio.*

Hallam, E. (Editor) (1986) – *The Plantagenet Chronicles*, Phoebe Philips & Macmillan Publishers.

Hardrada, Harald – *The Gamanvisur, Skaldic Verses*, Royal Library Sweden.

Harris, R. Rt. Rev. (1993) – *Art and Beauty of God*, Mowbray, London.

Heimskringla, Sweden.

Hicks, C. (1998) – *England in the 11th Century*, Stamford Press, USA.

Hill, R. (ed.) (1962) – *Gesta Francorum*, Nelson Medieval Texts, London.

James, E. (1988) – *The Northern World in the Dark Ages 400-900*, Oxford Illustrated History of Medieval Europe, UK.

James, M. R. (ed.) (1953) – *The Apocryphal New Testament*, Clarendon Press, UK.

Jerlow, L. G. (ed.) (1968) – *Ordo Niderosiensis Ecclesiae*, Oslo.

Jómsvíkingadrápa, Sweden.

Jómsvíkinga saga, Sweden.

Josephus (1981) – *The Jewish War* (trans. G. A. Williamson). Also Antiquities of the Jews.

Kelly's Handbook to the Titled, Landed and Official Classes, various years.

Kjeilen, T. (2006) – *LexiOrient – Nabateans.*

Kraeling, C. H. (1951) – *John the Baptist*, Schribner's Sons, London.

Lair, J. (1885) – Introductory notes to *Dudon de Saint-Quentian, Mémoires de la Société de Antiquitaires de Normandie.*

Le Loup, J-Y. (Trans.) (2003) – *The Gospel of Philip,* Inner Traditions, USA.

Le Loup, J-Y. (Trans.) (2002) – *The Gospel of Mary Magdalene,* Inner Traditions, USA.

Le Loup, J-Y. (Trans.) (2005) – *The Gospel of Thomas,* Inner Traditions, USA.

Levi, I. (1895) – *L'origine davidique de Hillel,* Revue des études juives, France.

Liber Hymnorum – MSS. E. 4,2; Trinity College, Dublin.

Lopes, A. (1997) – *The Popes,* Futura Edizioni, Roma.

Loud, G. A. (1981) – *Gens Normannorum,* Journal of Anglo-Saxon Studies, UK.

Maclagan, M. & Louda, J. (1999) – *Lines of Succession,* Little, Brown & Co.

MacQuitty, W. (1976) – *The Island of Isis,* Book Club Associates, London.

Malaterra, Gaufridus (c. 1098) – *Historia Sicula,* ed. Migne, Patrologia Latina.

Mander, A & R. (2002) – *The Black Madonna,* Published privately.

Martin, M. (1981) – *The Decline and Fall of the Roman Church,* G. P. Putnam's Sons, New York.

McFarlan, D. M. (2005) – *Dictionary of the Bible,* Geddess & Grosset.

McKitterick, R. (1983) – *The Frankish Kingdoms under the Carolingians,* Longman, UK.

McLynn, F. (1995) – *1066, The Year of the Three Battles,* Jonathon Cape, London, UK.

Medieval Source Book, Fordham University Center for Medieval Studies.

Montgomery, B. G. (1968) – *Ancient Migrations and Royal Houses,* Mitre Press, UK.

Montgomery, H. (2002) – *Montgomery Millennium,* Megatrend, Belgrade.

Montgomery, H. (2006) – *The God-Kings of Europe,* The Book Tree, San Diego, California.

Montgomery, H. (2007) – *The God-Kings of England*, Temple Publications, UK.

Morkot, R. G. (2000) – *The Black Pharaohs*, Rubicon Press.

Manuscript M/s. 481.51-100 – Yale University Collection of Rare Books and Manuscripts.

Munch, P. A. (1810-1863) – *Der Norske Folks Historie*, Sweden.

Muhammed, Abu J. (1972) – *Tasfir-Ibn-i-Jarir at Tabri*, Vols I-III, Kubr-ul-Mar Press Cairo.

Norwich, J. J. – *Byzantium*, Penguin Books.

Odericus Vitalis, *Origine de la Normandie*, Paris edition, 1920.

Odericus Vitalis, *Historia Ecclesiastica*, Macmillan.

Oleson, T. J. (1955) – *The Witanagemot in the Reign of Edward the Confessor*, English Historical Review (EHR), London, UK.

Olaf Tryggvasson's Saga, Sweden.

Oleson, T. J. (1953) – *Edward the Confessor's Promise of the Throne to Duke William of Normandy*, HER.

Oman, Sir Charles, (1991 Edition) – *History of the Art of War in the Middle Ages*, Vols. I, II, Greenhill Books.

Pagels, E. & King, K. L. (2007) – *Reading Judas*, Allen Lane.

Payne, R. (1984) – *The Dream and the Tomb*, Penguin.

Patai, R. (1990) – *The Hebrew Goddess*, Detroit.

Peterborough Chronicler, (c. 1070).

Platts, B. (1985) – *Scottish Hazard*, Vols. I & II, Proctor Press.

Pope, C. N. (2005) – *Herodian Identities of the New Testament Characters*, domainofman.com.

Powicke, Sir F. M. & Fryde, E. B. (1961) – *Handbook of British Chronology*, 2nd Edition, Royal Historical Society.

Poynder, M. – *Mary Magdalene* – awaiting publication.

Public Record Office M/s 101/387/25 m. 27.

Pükert, W. (1953) – *Aniane und Gellone*, Germany.

Raymond of Aguilers, (c. 1100) – *Historia Francorum qui ceperunt Jerusalem*, R. H. C. Occ.; Vol. III.

Revel, J. (1918) – *Historie des Normans*, Paris.

Runciman, Sir S. (1951) – *The History of the Crusades*, Vols. I-III, Cambridge University Press.

Sawyer, B. & P. (1993) – *Medieval Scandinavia from Conversion to Reformation*, c. 800-1500, UK.

Schimann, J. (1951) – *Samuel Hannagid, the Man, the Soldier, the Politician*, Jewish Social Studies.

Schneid, H. (1973) – *Marriage*, Keter Books, Jerusalem.

Schorim, Ben S. (1978) – *Mon frère Jésus*, Editions du Seuil.

Seawright, C. (2007) – *Set (Seth), God of Storms, Slayer of Apep, Equal to and Rival of Horus*, featurestories/set.htm.

Series Runica Prima, Danish State Archives.

Sinclair, Dr. H. – *Jesus' Family*, private papers in possession of Clan Sinclair Trust.

Smith, M. (1974) – *The Secret Gospel*, Gollancz.

Steenstrup, J. (1882) – *Normannerne*, Library B. G. Montgomery, Sweden.

Stoyanov, Y. (1994) – *The Hidden Tradition in Europe*, Penguin.

Swanton, M. (2000) – *Anglo-Saxon Chronicle*, Phoenix Press.

Szekely, E. B. (1996) – *The Gospel of the Essenes*, Daniel & Co. UK.

Szekely, E. & Weaver, P. (1986) – *The Gospel of Peace of Jesus Christ*, C. Daniel & Co. Ltd. UK.

Taylor, J. – *A Second Temple in Egypt*, Waikato University Press.

Taylor, J. (1967) – *Letters of Eleutherius to King Lucius*.

The Three Fragments, M/s. in the Burgundian Library, Brussels.

Thiering, B. (1992) – *Jesus the Man*, BCA, London.

Turner, L. (2006) – *Lectures in Egyptology*, Uttoxeter and District U3A.

Wace, R. (c. 1135) – *Le Roman de Rou*, (ed. A. J. Holden), 3 volumes, Soc. des Anciens Texts Français (1970-1973).

Wahlberg, E. (1913) – *Sur L'Origine de Rollon*, France.

William of Jumierges (c. 1130) – *Gesta Normannorum Ducum*.

William of Malmesbury (c. 1129) – *De gestis regum Anglorum*.

William of Poitiers (c. 1074-1077) – *Gesta Guillelmi Ducis*

Normannorum et Regis Anglorum.
William of Tyre, (c. 1200) – *Historia – Rerum in Partibus Transmarinis Gestarum*, R. H. C. Occ. IV. Also (c. 1108) – *Die Latinische Fortsetzung* (ed. Salloch 1934), Leipzig.
Worsac, J. (1863) – *Den danske Erobring af England og Nomanniet*, Denmark.

Yeatman, J. P. (1882) – *History of the House of Arundel*, Mitchell & Hughes.

Zosima, *Historia* – Private Copy.
Zuckerman, A. J. (1972) – *A Jewish Princedom in Feudal France 768-900*, Columbia University Press, USA.

Index

A

Abdias 15, 17, 19, 21-23, 25, 27, 29, 31, 41, 45, 46, 86, 93, 99, 178
  Bishop of Babylon 15
  Obadiah 15
  Petra Dynasty 15, 17, 19, 21-23, 25, 27, 29, 31
Acre 117, 119, 155
Acts of Thomas 31, 32, 41, 43, 178
Adhemar, Bishop of Le Puy 69, 75, 81
Akiba, Rabbi 48
Albigensian Crusade (See also Cathars) 115, 118, 126
Alexandria 7, 76, 118
Angevins 101
Anjou 98, 101, 103, 104, 115, 162
  Fulk Nerra 102
  Fulk, King of Jerusalem 98, 101, 102, 103, 117, 155, 162
  Gerald of Wales 101
  Melusine 41, 101, 102
Anna Comnena 73, 85, 180
Anna, Anne, Chana 22, 45
Ante-Nicene Fathers 8, 14, 178
Antioch 7, 69, 75, 77, 78, 80, 81, 87, 98, 102, 115
Anya 17, 31
Apep 112, 116, 184
Apulia 62, 64, 65, 70, 71
Arduin, Lombard 64
Aretas 17, 18
Arimathea 22, 47
Arius, Arian 8
Asherah 112
Athanasius 8

B

Baghdad 118, 160
Bagrat, Bagratide 77, 78
Baldwin I of Edessa & Jerusalem 87, 90, 93-95, 155
Baldwin II of Edessa & Jerusalem 90, 94-96, 98, 101, 155
Bar Kochba (Simon ben Cozeba) 48, 51
Barbelo 113
Bardaisan (See under Edessa) 41
Basil II 57
Benevento 62

Benjamites 51, 53
  Fighting Force 48, 51, 53, 54, 58
Bernard of Clairvaux 90, 96, 97, 99, 117, 121, 178
Bethany 11, 13, 14, 27-30, 33, 34, 37, 42, 51, 82, 98, 114, 117, 121, 124-127, 130, 180
  House of Bethany 11, 14, 82, 124, 125
  Mary, Miriam of 17, 24, 29, 42, 51, 52, 127
Black Prince 38
Bohemond of Taranto 70, 71, 73, 74, 76, 77, 81, 98
Boiaines, Catapan 62, 64
Boulogne 71, 84, 89, 90, 94, 95
Burgundy 30, 71, 93, 141

C

Caesarea 75, 181
Calabria 62, 64, 66, 70
Cannae 62, 63
Cathars 53, 115, 117, 118
Cleophas 25
Constantine 7- 9, 52, 62, 78, 92, 181
Council of Nicaea 92
  Mother Helen 8

D

Daimbert, Patriarch 83, 93
Dead Sea Scrolls 8, 16, 43, 91, 181
Desposyni: See under Jesus 7, 53
DNA 6, 10, 113, 123
  Jewish Cohen Haplotype 10, 14, 122, 124
  Sinclair Clan 10
Dorylaeum 74, 75
Duke of Normandy 63, 70, 71, 82, 93, 103

E

Edessa 15, 31, 41, 69, 77-80, 83, 89-97, 99, 102, 115, 180
Elchasai 52
Elchasaites 7, 52, 53, 55, 117
Elizabeth 25, 26, 28, 104
Elvira of Aragon 69
Ephesus 7
Essenes 16, 46, 184
Esser 16
Esther 42

Ethiopia 16, 17
  Aethiopia 17, 28
  Falashas 16
  Magdala 16, 17
Eusebius, Bishop of Caesaera 8, 14, 31, 91, 99, 180

F
First Crusade 61, 68, 69, 71-73, 75, 79, 81
Florence of Worcester 105, 107, 116, 180

G
Gaimer 62-64
Gethsemane 45, 47
Gherbod 120
God-Kings of England 7, 53, 54, 56, 61, 65, 69, 82, 85, 99, 104, 146, 183
God-Kings of Europe 7, 9, 10, 13, 15, 18, 24, 25, 29-33, 41, 42, 51, 53, 88, 105, 107, 110, 113, 114, 119, 183
Godfrey of Bouillon 83
Golden Legend 29, 30, 39, 127, 144
Gospel of Judas 113
Gospel of Luke 25, 47, 49
Gospel of Mary 46, 139, 182
Gospel of Mathew 8, 22, 110
Gospel of Philip 10, 14, 23, 93, 182
Gospel of Thomas 23, 31, 182
Guynemer 75, 76, 89

H
Haggadah 46, 49
Harald Gormsson (Bluetooth) 54
Harald Hardrada 58, 63, 181
Hautville 61, 63-66, 68
Hautvilles 63, 65, 71
Henry I of England 95, 101
Henry II, Emperor 103, 162
Herod 18, 22, 34, 84
Herodians 18, 33, 34
Holy Lance 77
Holy Land 69
Holy Mandylion 92
Horus 111-114, 116, 184
Housecarls 54
Hugh of Vermandois 70-73, 89
Hyksos 112
Hynlujóo, Icelandic Saga 113

I
Idumeans 22
Invasion of Sicily 67

J
James 7, 22, 23, 42, 51, 52, 93, 99, 180
  brother of Jesus 7, 92, 99, 180
  ha Rama 22
  Jacob 22-24, 28, 41, 42, 46, 52, 53, 124
Jerusalem 7, 15-17, 19, 22, 23, 45, 49, 53, 54, 62, 69-71, 80-98, 101-103, 115, 117, 120, 131, 137, 138, 155, 160, 162, 184
Jesus 2, 7-10, 12, 16-19, 22, 23-28, 31-34, 38, 41, 42, 45-52, 54, 79, 81, 83, 91-94, 99, 109, 113-115, 117, 125, 126, 160, 179, 180, 184
Jew 18
Jewish 10, 13, 18, 31, 46, 48, 49, 52, 53, 54, 82, 88, 92, 94, 101, 102, 124, 125, 180, 181, 184, 185
Joachim 23, 25
Joanna 23, 41, 42
John the Baptist 15, 16, 19, 25-28, 34, 45, 52, 109, 182
Joms-Vikings 51, 53-55, 57, 97, 117, 120
Josephus 18, 31, 140, 181
Julius Africanus 15
Jupiter (See under Virgin Birth) 8

K
Kassite Dynasty 112, 113, 163
Kerbogha 77, 78, 80
kings 1, 7-10, 12-16, 18, 20, 22, 24-26, 28-34, 36, 38, 41, 42, 46, 51-54, 56, 58, 61, 62, 64-66, 68, 69, 70-72, 74, 76, 78, 82, 84-86, 90, 92, 94, 96, 98, 99, 102, 104-108, 110, 112-116, 118, 119, 129, 131, 133, 135, 137, 139, 146, 155, 156, 169, 171, 179, 181, 183
Knights Templar 2, 58, 61, 89, 90, 92-94, 96, 117, 121, 159
Koinonum 10

L
Lamentations Raba 17
Lombardy 62

M
Maniakes, George 63
Mapa Mundi & Hereford Cathedral 96
Maria 7, 12, 42, 53, 54, 55, 67, 109, 114
Martha 12, 29, 121, 131-133
Marthana 12
Martin, Malachi 8, 14, 23-25, 31, 32, 49, 53, 56, 125, 158, 182
Mary 2, 8, 12, 13, 15, 17-19, 22, 23, 25-30, 33, 34, 37, 39, 42, 46, 51, 52, 114, 117, 121, 125-127, 130, 131-144, 182, 183
Matilda 72, 101, 103, 119, 120
    daughter of Henry I 103
    wife of William I 119
Melchizedek 45, 49
Melo 62, 64
Mercenary Companies 120
Meroveus, Merovech, Merovee, Merobald 126
Michael IV, Emperor 63
Miltiades 9
    Bishop of Rome 7, 9, 39
Minyan 46
Monte Siricolo 64
Montemaggiore 64
Muriel 26, 28, 125, 126
N
Nag Hammadi 10, 93
Naples 62
Nestorians 94
Nicaea 8, 73, 92
19th Dynasty 112
O
Ordericus Vitalis 69, 88
Osiris 111-114
Osmeus 12, 26-28, 125
    John Martinus or Matinus 26-28, 125
    son of Jesus and Mary Magdelene 26, 28, 125
P
Passover 16, 46, 47, 49
People's Crusade 69
Pessach 16, 46
Peter the Hermit 69

Petra 15-23, 25, 27-29, 31, 45, 93
Pharisaic 45, 52
Pharisee 52, 132
Pope Calistus II 93, 97
Pope Gelasius I 91
Pope Urban II 69
Poynder, M 34, 39, 183
R
Ra 111, 112
Rainulf "Drengot" and his brothers: 62-66, 153
    Asclettin 63, 65, 66, 154
    Gilbert 63
    Osmund 63, 65
Ravendel 78
Raymond IV of St. Gilles (Toulouse) 69, 72
Raymond of Aguilers 81, 85, 88, 184
Richard I of Capua 63, 154, 162
Robert of Normandy 72, 74, 80-83, 90, 95, 102, 103, 145
Robert, Count d'Eu 63
Rollo 63, 65, 72
Ruth 12, 27, 28, 51, 52, 125, 126
S
Saba 15, 16
Sabeans 15, 31
Sadducees, Sadduceen 45
Sahedic Coptic 10
Salome 18, 23, 41, 42
Samasota (Emirate) 78, 79
San Marco Argentano 66
Sarah, Sarah Bernice 26, 28, 33, 34
Seth 109-114, 116, 184
Sethians 113
Seti 111-113
Sheba 15, 16
Shroud of Turin 92
Sicarii 45
Sicily 61-63, 65, 67, 68, 70, 72, 115, 118, 154, 156
Simon 22, 23, 28, 41, 42, 45, 46, 48, 49, 131, 132, 156
    Zelotes 45, 49
Sorrento 62, 64
Spoleto 62
St. Clair, Sinclair 119, 146
    Sinclair 6, 10, 14, 25, 26, 28, 31,

32, 184
St. Maries de la Mer 33
St. Paul 76
Saul 33, 34, 49, 51, 109, 125
Sigismundus 12, 28, 109
Strut-Haraldsson 54
Stuart, Roderick 34
Sultan Arslan 74
Sweyn Forkbeard 54, 55
Sylvester 7, 9, 25, 32, 42, 52, 92
T
Taphnuz 79
Teutonic Knights 119, 157
    Ordenstaat 119
    Prussia 119, 158
Thaddeus 15, 41, 92, 93, 99, 102
Thera volcano 114
Thiering, Barbara 42, 46, 48, 125, 184
Thomas 23, 26, 28, 31, 32, 41, 43, 46,
91-93, 99, 102, 116, 124, 159, 178,
180, 182
    Didymus 23
Torah 18, 31, 94, 110
Turbessel 80
Tyrel, Walter 83
U
Ulvungar 6, 7, 10, 26, 55, 57, 61, 65,
71, 72, 75, 93, 95, 97, 98, 103, 109,
114, 115, 117-120, 154
Ulf 105-107, 109
V
Valois 37, 119
Varangians 57, 58, 59, 179
Venosa 64
Virgin Birth 8
Visigoths 7, 53, 55, 105, 106, 107
Vladimir of Kiev 57
W
Wends 54, 56, 57, 59, 178
William of Normandy 183
William of Tyre 82, 87, 89, 94, 99,
101, 102, 172, 186
Y
Yaghi-Siyan (Gov. of Antioch) 76
Z
Zacharias 23, 25
Zadokites 16, 45, 47
Zealots 16, 45, 47, 54

Zeus 8
Zokar 42

Lightning Source UK Ltd.
Milton Keynes UK
UKOW051426181111

182284UK00002B/47/P